ARCHITECTURE MAN IN POSSESSION OF HIS EARTH

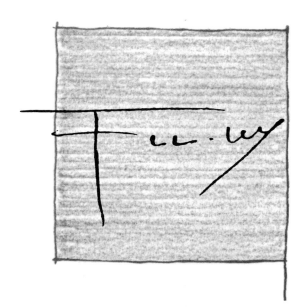

ARCHITECTURE

Doubleday & Company, Inc., Garden City, New York, 1962

MAN IN POSSESSION OF HIS EARTH

FRANK LLOYD WRIGHT

biography by IOVANNA LLOYD WRIGHT

designer and editor PATRICIA COYLE NICHOLSON

We would like to express especial gratitude, in the compilation of this work, to the many talented people of the Frank Lloyd Wright Foundation and the Taliesin Associated Architects. Their understanding assistance and knowledge have made possible the organization and publication of the Frank Lloyd Wright original renderings and the many valuable photographs available only in the Foundation archives.

The co-operation of Duell, Sloan and Pearce, Hastings House, and Horizon Press in allowing printing of certain photographs from their publications is much appreciated.

Finally, we are indebted to Enid Moore for her assistance in European research.

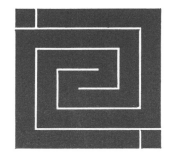

Books by Frank Lloyd Wright:

From the Horizon Press:

A TESTAMENT
THE NATURAL HOUSE
THE LIVING CITY (includes THE DISAPPEARING CITY and WHEN DEMOCRACY BUILDS)
THE STORY OF THE TOWER
THE FUTURE OF ARCHITECTURE
AN AMERICAN ARCHITECTURE
DRAWINGS FOR A LIVING ARCHITECTURE (edited by Edgar Kaufmann, Jr.)
FRANK LLOYD WRIGHT: WRITINGS AND BUILDINGS (edited by Edgar Kaufmann, Jr., and Ben Raeburn)

From Duell, Sloan and Pearce:

AN AUTOBIOGRAPHY
GENIUS AND THE MOBOCRACY
IN THE NATURE OF MATERIALS (compiled by Henry Russell Hitchcock)
ON ARCHITECTURE (edited by Frederick Gutheim)

Books about Frank Lloyd Wright:

From the Horizon Press:

THE STRUGGLE WITHIN by Olgivanna Lloyd Wright
OUR HOUSE by Olgivanna Lloyd Wright
THE SHINING BROW—FRANK LLOYD WRIGHT by Olgivanna Lloyd Wright

From Reinhold:

FIRST GOLDEN AGE by Grant Manson

CONTENTS

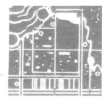

Allen Davison

Taliesin West—foundation, office, and home of Frank Lloyd Wright on the Maricopa mesa, near Phoenix, Arizona

Photograph of Frank Lloyd Wright, 1932

opening message

Building is a circumstance man shares with animals, birds, the fish and the insect. But architecture—great mother-art—begins where such creature-building leaves off and man's sovereignty—his spirit—reigns. Lower orders of life build by hereditary instinct: sea shells, bird-nests, the honeycomb of the bee, the citadel of the ant. All such creature-building is a gift by nature. In bewildering variety we find in lives of the creatures basis of earthly building long before man's civilization of himself began or ever could begin to appear, as architecture.

So, although architecture is building, this vast world of creature-building is not architecture. Well informed by heredity, its beauty is natural—for instance, the tortoise-shell fashioned by the awkward turtle. All creature-building is elemental and its beauty inevitable. We see this in the little sea-houses picked up on the seashore or found miraculously on the bottom of the sea. This creature-world builds with an elementary sense of unity circumscribed by the actual circumstances of its own life and environment. Beauty, then, is the consequence of innate gift. So we see the unity of *being,* with the forces that measure, determine and mature this gift of nature-building by heredity.

The plant also builds; growing from seed to root, stem and branch, in order to carry the exquisite flower and consequent fruit. The tree itself rises to majesty. Congruity, continuity and plasticity we see as qualities throughout all natural building. Beauty is due to some mystic innate-power elemental as life is to life itself. Harmony is organic and comes forth to the human eye. Everywhere creature-life is so lived and it appeals to our sense of the appropriate. We call this concordance beauty and we see it as a great gift of nature.

Man, though himself originally a nature-pattern like the antelope and the horse, seems to have had no such in-born building instruction. Man seems to be dependent upon inspiration from a higher source. Neither by heredity nor by instinct does man succeed in the life-beautiful. He seems to have missed much of this accord, concord and simplicity and instead left a trail of ugliness in his wake, instead of what we call this reality of nature—beauty. In all of man's attempted civilizations this natural right to beauty seems left to man's vision of himself and the affair seems to rest not so much in his education as in the culture of his spirit.

Not until the spirit of man becomes conscious of *need* for the benison of beauty *in his way of being* in order to sustain his soul and uplift his spirit as well as comfort and protect his body, does man himself seem to share the instinct for beauty with subordinate orders and forms of life. So man's building is largely the mere craft of the carpenter with his square. By using his multifarious sciences man is furnished and circumscribed until he awakens to the vision of the intrinsic truth of form. Then beauty comes to his rescue and we have architecture—the mother-art of human-kind. As a consequence we also see sculpture, painting and music.

Science may produce a civilization but not a culture. Man's life under science alone stays sterile. These crafts in essence are similar to that of the carpenter's square. Due to this, recourse in building is that of "the rectilinear frame of reference," his intellectual deduction by way of the carpenter. The engineer is a scientist, but however ingenious and inventive he may be, he is not a creative artist. He is without true reference to the form of organic harmonies to be found as the determining circumstance of man's creative life. Qualities that should characterize man and enable him to rise above his protoplasmic associates on earth seem rare—hard to come by. But man's great gift lies in his vision. Owing to over-reliance on science, too seldom is this vision turned inward toward the beauty of himself: man's own spiritual-haven. When vision does come into his being and as the mind of man takes hold of his destiny, beauty becomes a vital experience of great consequence to him. There and then, beyond the instincts of the lower orders of life on lower levels of being, we have man's creative architecture: the greatest proof of his immortal soul. To qualify his life on earth his art has more and more consciously grown out of his own spirit overcoming the obstructions by science of the circumstances of his earthly life. Man's necessities include the spiritual life and out of this his buildings as architecture grew, the very flower and fruit of human vision. Architecture lies deep as the basic culture of all civilizations, serving and served by the arts of sculpture, painting and music.

Through his architecture we shall see how man has triumphed over mere building during the past ages: see how ethnic eccentricities varied his vision and molded "style." Finally, we shall see how great changes in his life have developed his architecture as recorded by and for posterity.

In the animal kingdom we may see form always following function. But man sees form and function as one of the imaginative realm, where space is embodied in the world of form we call architecture. This is the greatest consequence of the life of art by mankind as man comes from his aboriginal cave on the way from his gods to God.

As man—the savage—emerges from the natural cave to build one of his own, origins of the history of architecture are lost in perspective. As he civilized himself he adorned these artificial caves as he set them upon the ground out under the sun. Soon after came buildings from the mind of man himself. He created space in which to live; not only protected from the elements but protected from his fellow man as well. But that was not enough—to live content, now civilized, he *meant* to make these cave-buildings beautiful. Then was architecture born.

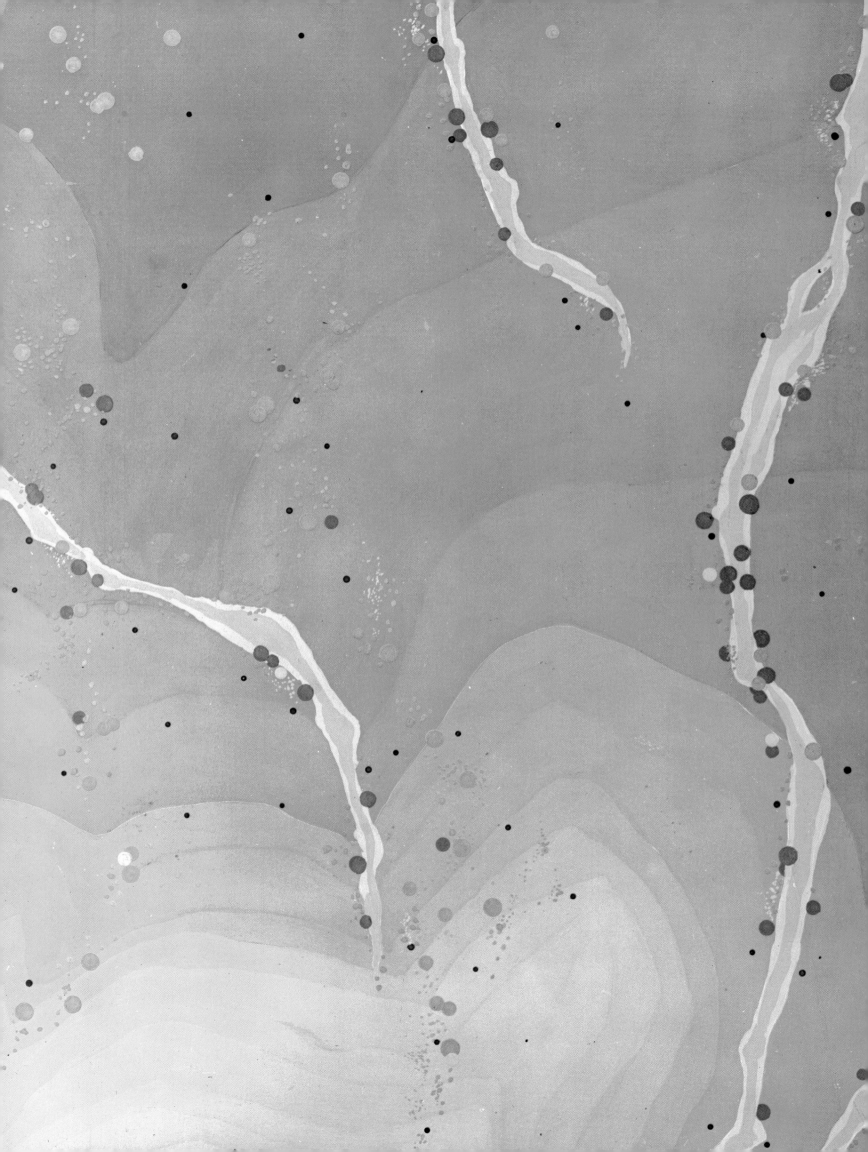

Plan view of Taliesin West

MY FATHER — FRANK LLOYD WRIGHT

by IOVANNA LLOYD WRIGHT

The heredity of Frank Lloyd Wright was as powerful as the circumstances in which he grew. His Welsh grandfather, Richard Lloyd-Jones, was a self-declared preacher of the Unitarian faith and a maker of the tall, conical Welsh hats by trade. He had married a Welsh woman of aristocratic birth—Mary Lloyd—and had joined her name with his. Although she wedded him against the protests of her family, she loved him enough to endure the hardships that his search for freedom and truth would bring to them. In 1845 they left Wales and arrived in the United States. They brought their family of seven to this new land which was the promise of justice, freedom, and a man's right to be himself. Richard's was a fiery spirit, and Isaiah his favorite prophet.

The family traveled halfway across the United States to Wisconsin by boat and covered wagon. When at length they reached Ixonia, a tiny community in southwestern Wisconsin, they settled down for six years. During this time four more children were added to the Lloyd-Jones clan. But Richard's impassioned Unitarian preaching was considered radical by the staid settlers there. His fiery force within drove him to search for new places where he could go on with his work. The family gathered their belongings once again and moved further up the Wisconsin River. Here Richard found a green, luxuriant valley reminiscent of their native Wales. Gently sloping hills covered with virgin forests melted into fields of fertile, dark earth. Springs and streams were abundant—all winding into the sand-cliffed river. Indians still lived there and welcomed these Wisconsin pioneers with friendship. Richard, now satisfied, his eldest sons by his side, built the family a clapboard, shingled cabin, and the far-spreading forests began to give way. Richard and his family continued in their struggle for existence while the farm grew and prospered.

Gradually more settlers were added to the green valley to make their homes and farms. With a Bible held under his arm, Richard would ride from farm to farm preaching on Sundays, until, with the help of the now greatly enlarged community, he built his first chapel. The Druid crest that Richard carved on the newly hewn rock at the entrance symbolized "Truth against the World."

*   *   *

The valley in Wisconsin
where the Wright family settled

Allen Davison

Daughter Anna Lloyd-Jones was five years old when the family left Wales. She spent her girlhood in the Valley as a teacher, riding horseback through the rough, unbroken country to a small schoolhouse. She was loved by her pupils, who referred to her as "Sister Anna." Anna's love for and belief in education exceeded even her love of nature.

At twenty-nine she met a handsome, distinguished-looking gentleman from the East—William Russell Cary Wright, a relative of the poet James Russell Lowell. An intellectual from Hartford, Connecticut, he had been educated at Harvard University, where he studied medicine and law. But he discovered that his love of music and literature was stronger than the acquired knowledge of law or medicine, and descending from a long line of ministers himself, he also had a deep interest in religion. Now he became a circuit rider—a preacher-musician who rode from town to town teaching singing and composition. He and Anna met at a gay song fest and fell in love. He fulfilled her dream of a finely educated gentleman, and he, a widower of forty-six, was charmed by her spirited Welsh beauty. Shortly thereafter they were married.

During her first pregnancy Anna was determined that she would have a boy and that he would be a great architect. And on June 8, 1869, in the village of Richland Center, in Wisconsin, Anna gave birth to a son. The father, a patriot and romanticist, wanted to call his boy Frank Lincoln Wright. But the mother insisted upon the family name of Lloyd, and being Welsh and strong of mind, she won—he was called Frank Lloyd Wright—"Free Pure Maker."

Anna was strong-willed and unwavering in her decisions. If her son were to be a great architect he must have the best, the finest that she could possibly provide for him. She believed in pre-natal influences and had often looked at beautiful pictures—of cathedrals, sculpture, and paintings. She loved to listen to good music and spent much time walking in the fields and hills gathering wild flowers. And after the birth of her precious infant she had hung in his room wood engravings of the most beautiful cathedrals, which she had bought for him. She created imaginative flower arrangements in the house and added whatever objects the poor family could afford; possessing an artistic sense, she placed them where they were most pleasing to the eye.

Through her son's early years she was untiring and attentive to the last detail of his surroundings—even his food. As he grew into childhood, he was allowed no candy, no white bread, no cake; nothing that was considered "unnatural" was ever found on her family table. She had little trust in medicine. In later years her son used to tease her: "Mother, all you care about is whole-wheat bread and religion." But he adhered to these rigorous rules all his life.

*   *   *

The few years that the minister's family spent in the Valley grew leaner. There was not much interest in culture among the hard-working country people. Thinking that the more intellectual atmosphere of the East would lend itself better to his calling, William Wright moved his little family back to Weymouth, Massachusetts. They settled in a small wooden house and William preached in a nearby church, now earning his bread as a Baptist minister. Anna saw to it that her son attended the best private school. They lived chiefly by the kindness of their neighbors—often there were donations.

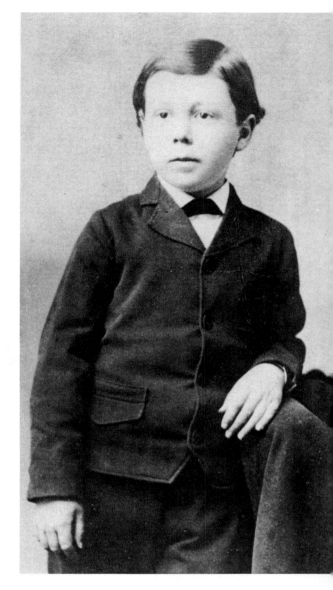

Frank Lloyd Wright at age 10

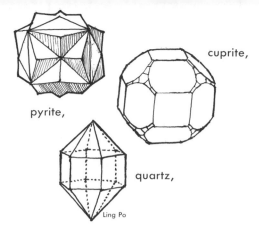

pyrite,

cuprite,

quartz,

Ling Po

Mineral crystals

John Amarantides

Chambered nautilus shell

Section of chambered nautilus shell

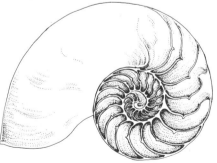

Ling Po

Section through
West Indian chalk shell

But despite the outward conditions of poverty, the development of the son continued. His father insisted that he spend long hours listening to good music and learning to understand the way in which it was constructed. As the boy lay awake at night listening to his father play, it seemed to him that sounds could take shape and make various forms—all connected with one another. Music became to him "an edifice of sound."

When young Frank was seven years old he assisted his father at church, pumping the air in the back room for the huge organ while his father played Bach. He would push and pull the bellows until his small back and arms hurt him so he cried from pain. Once he broke down and his father brought him home to an indignant mother. More and more often the father and mother disagreed as to the upbringing of their son. All the mother's love and attention was transferred from her husband to her son. William Wright felt this deeply and began to withdraw from his family into his work. But, according to his strict methods of teaching, his son was learning to play the piano, to draw and to paint, learning to read fine literature. His mother often read him poetry in the evenings.

Once, at the Exposition Building in Philadelphia, she came across a brilliant exhibition of children's toys—a collection of various geometric forms and shapes made out of wood, paper, and other materials. These, she discovered, belonged to the Friedrich Froebel Kindergarten system. Froebel was an innovator who had worked out a method for young children whereby they could learn the nature of various forms and colors—the myriad ways in which they might be combined to create designs. Anna took lessons from one of Froebel's representatives in order to teach his system and the games that were devised to strengthen and expand an instinct for harmonious design.

Froebel did not believe in imitating nature by representative drawing. He taught the principle of geometry underlying all natural form, as in the snowflake, the shell, the crystal—various petals and leaves where clear abstract pattern and mathematical construction unfold under close study. These "gifts" of Froebel's disclosed an actual unit system in all nature, the principle of which architect Wright applied to plans he created in later life.

Many years after, Frank Lloyd Wright spoke of his first experiments with form—with the straight line, the flat plane, the square, the triangle, and the circle. The square modified by the triangle produced the hexagon; the circle modified by the straight line would make an octagon. Adding thickness, the square could become a cube, the triangle a tetrahedron, the circle a sphere; these elemental forms are the basis of all the world's architecture.

* * *

Two new members made their appearance in the minister's family—first a daughter, Jane, and later another daughter, Maginel. . . . Time passed, the needs of the children grew, and the severe conditions of poverty increased. Anna longed to go back to Wisconsin. She prevailed upon William, and in 1880 they moved to Madison, the capital of the state. Anna had noticed a predisposition to dreaminess in her fast-growing son. But she also thought she knew the cure for it and wrote to her brother James, who owned a large farm in the Valley, asking if he would take her eleven-year-old boy to help with the farm work. James gladly accepted, and traveled the forty miles to Madison by wagon to take his young nephew home with him. From then

Snow crystals

Allen Davison

Waterfall in valley looking toward Uncle James' farm

on the boy worked during springs and summers in the country and returned to a public school in Madison in the autumn.

*   *   *

The following five years spent at his uncle James' farm were the most decisive in the pliant, forming nature of the young Frank Lloyd Wright. Through all his later life he went back often in reminiscence to these early days of hardship, which held also the romance and beauty of his boyhood. Here he learned the principle of hard work on which he built his life.

Young nephew Frank adhered strictly to the rules of his uncle's house. He rose at four o'clock every morning. He walked barefoot over the hills, the rocky ridges, and muddy streams to bring in the cows for milking. He cut paths with a sickle and scythe through the dark, overgrown woods. In the high heat of summer, in heavy rains and winds, he learned to mend fences, drive the wild sows out of the gardens, butcher hogs and chickens, kill cows for their meat and skin them for their hides, and milk the large herd morning and evening. He worked in his bare feet shoveling wagonloads of manure, pitching hay, bringing in the corn shocks, plowing—until his fingers bled, the palms of his hands grew hard and sinewy from the handles of the sickle and the hoe. He learned to "add tired to tired, and then add it again and again." He learned the nature of the earth as it woke in spring, and as the mysterious forces of life lay silent but alive, wrapped in the white death of winter. He felt the current of life underlying all things and found that nature had a rhythm he could feel as strongly and clearly as he felt rhythm in a great symphony.

Uncle James

Sometimes, too tired to sleep after a day's work, he would rise at night in the full of the moon and walk over the stony ridges to his favorite hill. There he would sit for hours—thinking and dreaming. Why had Grandfather preached: "The flower fadeth, and the grass withereth, but the Word of the Lord endureth forever . . ."? He remembered the patriarchal figure as he preached to the bowed heads of his congregation. Were not the flowers and the grass the Word of God incarnate? When they died, new ones—often different and more beautiful ones—took their places. Was not the Word of God also the Work of God? Was it not man's place to live in harmony with the beauty that was of God's own making? He thought of the rock stratas that were built into the hills. And in all the marvels and miracles he had learned of he began to see a plan.

Hillside School near Spring Green, Wisconsin,
built in 1902 and added to in 1956

Sandak

John Amarantides

Rock strata and pool

Uncle Enos

Thus the springs and summers passed. Once, when he was still very young, tired beyond endurance, he tried to run away. He struck out over the hills to the river, where he planned to take the ferry boat to Madison. He arrived at sundown and sat on the edge of the boat dangling his legs in the dark waters. Miserable and half regretting what he had done, he was still determined not to give up when he suddenly felt someone standing near him. He looked up and saw the tall figure of Enos—youngest and gentlest of his uncles. "Where are you going, Frank?" The boy did not answer. He looked down at his hands. They were blistered and bleeding where brambles had torn the skin. Tears fell in dusty streaks down his face. "Yes, I know," Uncle Enos said, and his voice was kind. "It's hard for a boy to grow into a man. First he has to learn to work and suffer like a man. Learn to work the soreness out by keeping right on working. You will grow stronger, Frank, by staying with it, no matter how much it hurts. Keep right on even when you are stiff and tired and discouraged. And by keeping on you will see that you can do almost anything and never feel it too much. Someday you will be so strong that you can laugh like your uncle James and never be afraid of anything. Work is a challenge that creates strong men and roots out the weak ones." The words rolled like faraway thunder through the boy's ears. They pulsed with the blood through his veins—through his aching, weary body. "Work is a challenge that creates strong men and roots out the weak ones." The eleven-year-old looked up at the dignified man with the brown beard and soft gray eyes. Enos put his arm around the boy's thin, small shoulders. They walked up the bank, the boy coming reluctantly. Uncle Enos lifted him onto his horse, and together they rode back to the farm.

*　　*　　*

Determined to become an architect, Frank Lloyd Wright at the age of sixteen entered the University of Wisconsin at Madison. It was 1885. There was no adequate course in architecture, so he enrolled in the engineering class, thinking to gain at least some practical experience. He had saved what he could at the farm out of nineteen dollars a month in wages. His mother had sold a few belongings to help him through college—an ancestral gold Swiss watch, leather-bound books, some of the scant furnishings in their home. The family still had a meager income barely able to take care of essentials. And the relationship between father and mother steadily grew worse: William Cary Wright, proud, sensitive, and artistic, but unlucky, felt miserable in his failure to support them, and his inferiority complex made for further damage. His wife told him that he might leave them whenever he chose. In the same year that his son entered the university the father left his family and never returned. From the very first, the son had been especially devoted to his mother. Now, in this difficult time, he tried to bring in a little money by working as a draftsman for the dean of engineering, A. D. Conover. According to Wright, he learned more from this practical experience than in all the years of his formal education.

His best friend was Robert Lamp, whom he had met at public school. Robie's legs were withered; he walked on crutches. Frank was impressed by the boy's courage in accepting his misfortune. Their friendship had started when Frank rescued Robie from a group of boys who had taken his crutches away and were tormenting him. Their time together was happy and fruitful. While they still were in their teens, they constructed a printing press, designing different kinds of type. The prosperous father of another companion had provided money for their new adventure. Later, Robie asked Frank to design and build for him his first small cottage. The two were loyal friends until Robie's untimely death not many years later.

During Wright's sojourn in Madison, he witnessed the collapse of the State Capitol Building. Tragedy entered the lives of hundreds because the architect of the capitol had left its construction almost entirely to the contractor. Wishing to economize as much as possible, the contractor had filled the hollow supporting piers for the inside of the building with broken brick and stone. The piers were so rotted at the core that they could not support the enormous weight of the building; all the floors of the new wing crashed inward. The memory of mangled men half buried in blood-soaked rubble remained forever with Frank Lloyd Wright. He saw then of what importance it is for an architect to look after his own building to the last detail.

After three and one half years at the university, he was convinced that he was deriving no benefit from the limited, formalized education. His imaginative, creative mind was being impeded instead of liberated, and he wasted no time in his decision to leave the university. Against the wishes of his mother, the young man left Madison to find a job in Chicago.

* * *

He arrived in the city in drizzling rain with three dollars and eighty cents in his pocket. He wandered among the crowds, amazed at electric lights, which he had never before seen—the untidy, sign-spattered ugliness of the big city. He knew no one there except preacher Jenkin Lloyd-Jones, who was opening a new church at Lincoln Center. But the young man would not ask his uncle's help. He made the rounds of several architectural offices, asking for a job as a draftsman, with no luck. For three days he wandered through Chicago streets until he had so little money left that he was barely able to pay the bill of a cheap hotel—after which he simply tightened his belt. On the morning of the fourth day he decided to try the office of Lyman Silsbee, a fashionable Chicago architect who was designing his uncle's All Souls Church. A friendly looking man, Cecil Corwin, greeted him and took his drawings to the office. After a very short interview Silsbee accepted him on tracer's wages—eight dollars a week. He worked in Silsbee's office a little over a year, and then left him for another firm. However, finding out that he was not yet fit to work on large commissions, he returned to Silsbee.

Roofs of Taliesin in 1911

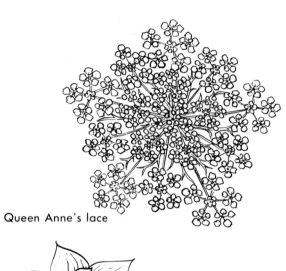

Queen Anne's lace

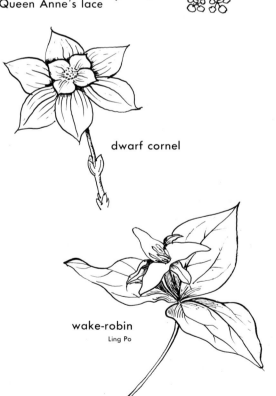

dwarf cornel

wake-robin
Ling Po

In Corwin he found a rare comrade. They loved to stay up far into the night, reading aloud from the New Testament. They often quoted passages to each other, discussing and applying them to their own time. Young Wright was an intense reader and was deeply affected by the literary masters. He also was much absorbed with the construction of words and ideas.

*   *   *

For two years the aspiring architect had been working hard and earning little at Silsbee's office. He asked for a raise and was refused. At that time the firm of Adler and Sullivan was becoming the most prominent in Chicago. Dissatisfied with Silsbee's low wages, he decided to leave and went to see Louis Sullivan, whose buildings he already knew and greatly admired.

The minister's son had a proud bearing. His features were finely drawn but strong. He had deep set brown eyes, a full mouth and thick, dark hair, worn a little longer than was the style of the day. There was a majesty about him which impressed Sullivan. After looking at the young man's drawings he said, "Wright, you have a good touch—you will do."

Sullivan's was the most revolutionary work in architectural design in the country. One of his valuable contributions to American architecture was his new image of the skyscraper. At that time a tall building was constructed as a series of boxes one on top of another, heavy in effect and giving no real sense of height. But Sullivan's flowing vertical lines, the soaring light and shadow patterns, emphasized the feeling of height with a sense of beauty. Apprentice Wright admired the master's beautiful freehand drawings, his sketches for trees, foliage, and flowers. But to the growing architect, the medium of T square and triangle was more in keeping with the geometry of nature and the essence of architecture. He would combine, in his own drawings for Louis Sullivan, this straight-line geometry with Sullivan's own ornamental, efflorescent line. Wright swiftly absorbed this artistry and recognized in Sullivan a man who believed in architecture. In this apprenticeship he saw an honest relationship whereby the apprentice was free to learn and absorb, yet retain his own individuality. He worked closely with his master, often staying with him in the office until late hours of the night.

Along with his successful rise in the drafting room, keen jealousy was aroused in his fellow draftsmen. They teased, ridiculed, and needled him. Boxing at the time was a favorite sport among them, and knowing the minister's son had no experience, they often invited him to fight. He secretly took boxing lessons, and when he thought he was ready to fight, he challenged two of them. He took on one, then another, and beat up both men. Outraged at the defeat, a draftsman began to jeer and mock him during lunch hours, when most of the

Chicago Architectural Photo Co.

Schiller Building—completed in 1892 by Frank Lloyd Wright's mentor Louis Sullivan

Transportation Building—Chicago World's Fair, 1893, Adler and Sullivan, Architects

Chicago Architectural Photo Co.

officials were out of the drafting room. One day Wright, insulted beyond endurance, hit the man squarely on the jaw. Another turned on him with a knife and stabbed him five times in the back, luckily missing his spinal column. Wright got the knife out of his hand and knocked him down again—as a friend of his came between them. Although he suffered from the knife wounds, the incident was never again mentioned. Wright won such confidence that Sullivan gave him an office adjacent to his own with a staff of thirty draftsmen working under his supervision.

His apprenticeship with Sullivan lasted for seven years. During this period he met Catherine Tobin, from Oak Park, and about a year later they were married. By terms of a contract with Adler and Sullivan the young husband borrowed money to design and build a small house in Oak Park. Their first son, Lloyd, was soon born to them. Later came John, Catherine, David, Frances, and Llewellyn. In critical need of money to support the increasing family, the young father now accepted commissions for houses. But when Louis Sullivan discovered the independent work he was displeased that Wright had taken the initiative without his permission. The two parted in 1893.

John Amarantides
Wild columbine

*　　*　　*

Frank Lloyd Wright opened his first independent office in the Schiller Building in Chicago with his long-time companion, Cecil Corwin. His first client was a River Forest resident, H. W. Winslow. Completed in 1893 the Winslow home was an absolute break with the traditional architecture of the time. It was copied by architects everywhere and gained renown in Europe. Simple strength, emphasis on the horizontal plane, the broad-sloping, extended eaves, direct use of Roman brick; the house began a new era in architecture and was the preamble to the great prairie homes that were to follow in the next five years. It showed, at such an early age in the architect's career, mastery in the handling of materials and design proportion.

The Winslow house caused a furor in River Forest. People came by the hundreds to see it, talk about it, admire or ridicule it. Daniel H. Burnham, a well known architect, was a friend of Winslow's who often visited the house and highly praised it. Burnham believed that Greek architecture could never be surpassed, that America was headed in the direction of classical art—as represented in the Chicago World's Fair of 1893, which, he was convinced, exerted tremendous influence over the cultural tastes of the country. Burnham and another wealthy neighbor of his, Ed Waller, offered Wright permanent security if he would go to study at the Beaux Arts in Paris for four years, then to Rome for two, all expenses paid for himself abroad and for his family at home. This offer was made on the condition that Wright would agree to study

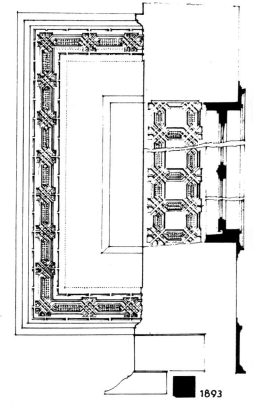
1893
Winslow house—detail

Drawing of Winslow house—Frank Lloyd Wright's first opportunity to design a house reflecting his independent thought, 1893

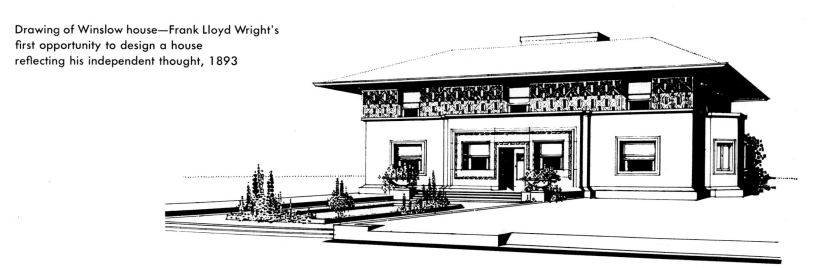

Tower Romeo and Juliet—
Taliesin, Wisconsin, 1896

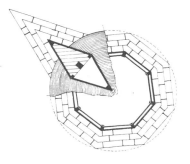

Plan of Tower Romeo and Juliet

carefully first, then design and build in the traditional, classical style. Waller and Burnham promised Wright that he would be secure for his lifetime—all he had to do was follow the rules and proceed as they directed.

The rebel architect was embarrassed. He did not like to disappoint the two men who had befriended him. Also, he was suffering under heavy debts, although always providing his family with beautiful surroundings. He told the two men that even Sullivan himself regretted the time he had spent at the Beaux Arts. He told them he could not go back on all his training—on all he had fought for and believed in now. He did not agree that the world was going in the direction of Greek architecture. The thought of it struck him like the thought of jail. The two men were amazed at his refusal and disappointed. They pressed him further, once more emphasizing the security of his future. Again he politely but firmly refused their offer.

*　　*　　*

Many and varied projects began to fill the young architect's office. From his aunts of the Hillside Home School in the Valley came a request for a windmill tower. It was to be built on a hill overlooking the school and the Valley. They did not want the customary skeleton-steel structure and had turned to their nephew for a different concept. Shortly they received the perspective sketch of their new tower. He called it Romeo and Juliet. The problem at hand was prevailing southwest winds and storms. A deep stone foundation, reaching into the ground as roots, anchored steel rods that rose to uphold a super-structure of wood siding bolted to these rods. Under adverse winds the tower would "give"—flexible enough to yield and sway with storms, free to return perfectly vertical as before in the calm. This was a pioneering idea in engineering-architecture, and the idea was enthusiastically received by his aunts.

Great excitement was caused by the first severe southwester in the Valley. Doubtful neighbors hurried to their doorways in view of the hill the next morning to see the tower lying destroyed, but they looked up and saw its slender structure unharmed in the clear summer morning. For sixty-five years Romeo and Juliet has weathered the worst midwestern storms. It stands today as when it was built, gently commanding the valley that lies around it.

*　　*　　*

Romeo and Juliet rose upon the American scene in a pastoral Wisconsin valley four years before the turn of the century—to herald a powerful new structural idea that this young architect was to expand brilliantly. In this tower, architecture finally became flexible, using the nature of plastic form in place of rigid buildings. A great hotel would rise and survive the most violent earthquakes because of this principle of flexibility and continuity.

The turn of the century saw America still asleep in Victorian tradition. America had not yet developed a culture of her own. The traditional American home of that time was a slipshod collection of styles and tastes then fashionable—the foam of different cultures of the past washed up onto the shores of the New World. The architect of this era was not much more than a selector who was chosen by his clients to put together various tastes and wrap them up in one package. A typical instruction from an architect of the time to his draftsman: *Take down design No. 42, put an English Tudor entry on the front, and add a Spanish patio in the back yard. We must please the client.*

Young architect Frank Lloyd Wright felt that the new home for the new country could never be a combination of variable tastes and dated European fashions. He loved the broad-sweeping motion of the midwestern prairie and felt that the homes built on this ground must belong to that great simplicity. Instinctively he knew that the need for shelter should also fulfill the finer human need for beauty: a home not only must belong to its place and time but should create a world in which the inhabitant can find the most noble elements of living.

Wright believed that the architecture belonging to the prairie must be based upon the simplicity of the horizontal line; and the homes he now designed were characterized by the broad, long, low-pitched roofs that expanded the sense of free space. The prairie home reached out in horizontal movement— the direct opposite of contemporary structures that were tilted up on end, restraining and confining the space within. His walls, porte-cocheres, terraces, balconies, roof lines, eaves, all became merged together in one unbroken whole or stream of line. Architect Wright at this early stage of his career coined the word "streamlined."

Because the home should be shelter for man against the worst elements of nature, it should also become the opportunity in which the most beautiful natural aspects could be enjoyed and lived in. The very walls of traditional homes were the confines of boxes, cut and punched with necessary holes for doors and windows. Interiors were totally cut off from the out-of-doors. But architect Wright saw that walls could be as plastic as screens. Broad stone masses—chimneys, walls, and piers throughout the plan—could do the work of carrying floors and roofs, leaving external walls free to be harmoniously arranged. These could also become screens of glass windows and glass doors opening outward, inviting views of gardens and beautiful landscapes wherever possible. Thus, the outside environs became closely related to the interior.

A new and different way of life was opened to the families who grew up in the Prairie Homes, a life of terraces and gardens, of abundantly spacious yet simple rooms. Gone were the clichés of Victorianism—dormers, gables, wasted heights—and the traditional damp cellar. In its place came a spacious room on the ground floor that gave access to those terraces and gardens. He eliminated the high-pitched roof with its sharp, narrow chimneys and dark attics. He replaced the typical fake fire grate of the day, artificially inserted in a papered wall, with deep-set wide fireplaces of sculptured masonry. He loved this sense of the fire burning deep in the very masonry of the house.

The old cubiclelike chambers he opened and freed into one gracefully flowing interior yet containing private rooms for the household. The customary parlor now became a great living space—often with dining room

Frank Lloyd Wright, 1903

Interior Robie house—prime example of prairie design (also see page 84)

Line drawing of Willitts house by Frank Lloyd Wright—Highland Park, Illinois, 1902

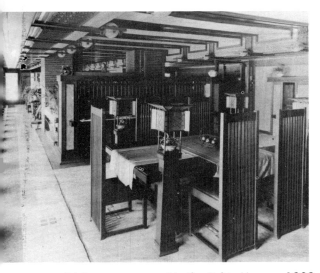

Dining arrangement in the Robie House—1909

Coonley Playhouse, 1908

Coonley house, detail—Riverside, Illinois

and library combined. Most important was the concept that the inner space of a building is the soul of that building—the exterior should grow out of the nature of the space within to be lived in. As the structure of a tree flows from roots to trunk to branches in one sweep of connectedness, so the new house and new conception of architecture maintained continuity from the central core foundations to every extending terminal.

Florid, rococo decor of the era gave way to architect Wright's organic idea of plasticity in simple, elegant form. The ornamentation then in vogue was an overgrown mass—a parasite on materials whose natural qualities had ceased to exist. He had furniture built on the straight-line pattern and kept all furnishings in scale with the house and belonging to the character of its design. Wood, long painted and carved beyond recognition, was now presented in its own soft warmth, its natural grain. Flowered wallpapers and garish paints were stripped away to reveal the natural eloquence of each material. Plaster and stucco came to have texture and were dyed in the process of their mixing to give full earth colors. Stone, with its weight and feeling of strength, was allowed to rise in wide chimney piers and extend as protecting walls and terraces. Brick, the product of the kiln, was revealed in its baked terra-cotta colors—the horizontal lines of the joints now an artistic feature. And glass, the transparent shield, merged, wherever desired, the interior with the outside world.

Ornamentation now came forth in the nature of the materials from which it was molded. Architect Wright used ornament as an integral flowering of structure. He saw that the machine could be a useful tool in the hands of the artist, and that it could faithfully render the beauty of his designs. Metal and glass together in straight-line patterns became delicate and subtle abstractions for windows, often set with opalescent and iridescent glass to give a play of jewel-like colors.

Wright knew the principle underlying all structure. Whichever material he chose served the nature of the structure he built and fulfilled the character of the material he used. This idea, ignored in architecture for hundreds of years, he called "In the Nature of Materials."

This, then, became the elemental principle of his architecture: Any building should first serve man and the purpose for which it is built. It must be true to the nature of its site and environment and to the nature of the materials of which it is composed. Above all, architecture must be true to the principle of unity, the timeless element of beauty that lives in all great works of art. This continuity of the relative parts to the whole, in plan and in elevation, in main structure and in detail, the architect conceived, developed and later called "Organic Architecture."

* * *

From his endlessly creative imagination one expression of this eternal principle followed upon another: the famous Prairie Homes rose on the midwestern plains, marking these vast prairies as the birthplace of an American culture. American architecture had acquired a character that the New World could rightfully call its own. Europe first awakened to Frank Lloyd Wright in 1910, when Berlin published a comprehensive elephant folio of his work. Architects everywhere abroad admired and copied him. But many more years were to pass before his own country would recognize his genius.

View of Coonley house from pool

There are few aspects of today's contemporary architecture, from open planning to wide overhanging roof, that cannot trace their inception to this work. The Ward W. Willitts house, the Heurtley, Heath, Tomek, Coonley, and Robie, along with thirty-five other houses built over a ten-year period, became roots of modern architecture.

Along with his designs for homes and with the perfecting of each succeeding plan came another significant advance, this time in public architecture. Barren of creative, imaginative designs, architects had piled imitation upon imitation. Banks were made to look like Greek temples. Libraries and public institutions copied the Colosseum, the Parthenon, the Roman Forum. Beneath all this stone crustation stolen from various epochs was buried the twentieth-century product of steel reinforcing. Glass, electricity, heating, and plumbing could make a Parthenon "practical." Architecture had been lost as an instructive and creative art. "Indeed, if the Greeks had had steel and glass, we would not have to think for ourselves at all," observed Wright.

The Larkin Administration Building for Buffalo, New York, was called by Frank Lloyd Wright the Affirmative Protestant. The building itself, in its noble simplicity, was its own sufficient ornament. Because it was to be built in a crowded industrial section of Buffalo, the architect's first idea was that the occupants of this building must be protected against the poisonous fumes of trains and factories. With all the glass areas sealed, he invented the system of bringing in air cleaned and cooled through huge filters: the first instance of air conditioning. With this office building came the first use of all-metal office furniture, the first example of wide plate-glass doors, the first modern wall-hung water closet. Brick was the feature material and was characteristically rendered. This edifice of 1904, when details were published in Europe, exerted vast influence upon the European architects' use of all materials—particularly of brick.

Most modern architecture issues from these early projects: but with the exception that while Wright himself moved on into unexplored fields and forms of expression, other architects continued to imitate only this early phase of his

Japanese print—Ichiryusai Hiroshige—
Frank Lloyd Wright Collection

work. The influence of his early work was eventually divided and interpreted by them into the reverse of his initial principles. Today we know of this negative interpretation as the International Style. A typical Victorian building was essentially a box, with effects and appendages applied onto it. The Internationalists believe that they began a new school, whereas in reality their design factories manufacture other kinds of boxes, often the glass box—totally stripped of any organic element of design. While all Wright's structure and ornament grew abundantly out of the nature of his sense of building, the imitators transformed his principle of simplicity into sterility. His belief in the machine as a tool in the hands of the artist, they reversed, to make the human being a slave to his own invention. To the Internationalist, man must conform: Man lives, thinks, and acts by the machine—therefore houses must be made into "machines for living."

*   *   *

Frank Lloyd Wright continued to move ahead with revolutionary ideas. Two years after the Affirmative Protestant, in 1906, he took another giant step—this time in church architecture. It was of poured-concrete construction and again emphasized the reality of interior space. For decades the architects have drawn inspiration from Unity Temple, standing now on a busy avenue in Oak Park, Illinois. The customary approach to liturgical design had been a rectangular box with a high steeple. Architect Wright wanted a stronger, more simple expression. He wished for a simple, noble room that could offer man prayer and meditation in a moving atmosphere. It was this sense of the noble room that became the core of Unity Temple.

The clients needed a church that would house a large congregation and yet be economical. Concrete was then used chiefly for cellars, warehouses, and garages. But now it became the architect's natural solution—he saw it as a magnificently finished surface. To save on the expense of form work, the four sides of the building would be identical, the roof a reinforced slab of poured concrete carried by four massive piers inside the room itself. With these things in mind, the architect created a great square room, with skylight perforations in the slab roof, and concrete walls that rose up to meet a continuous band of glass windows high above the street as protection from noise. This room was to be the essence of the church and would establish the character of the entire building. Related details would now develop from within. Separated from this great room by a low entrance foyer would be the congregational hall for banquets and meetings, with provisions for screening it into smaller rooms for Sunday school.

Unity Temple developed the concept that the interior space of a building is its true significance. Later he discovered that the Chinese philosopher Lao-tse had said about 600 B.C. that "the reality of a building does not consist in the four walls and the roof, but in the space within, which is to be lived in." The young architect was building this idea as a living part of man's everyday life, in his home, his office, and his place of worship. The space within is now free and plastic. Everywhere within, one plane flows into another, one area merges with another. There is no longer any feeling of two unrelated aspects, interior and exterior, for now they are one spirit interfused. Every part is fully related to the whole and expresses the purpose of the building. Despite constant doubts from members of the congregation during construction, after the new building was completed Wright received hundreds of messages telling him how pleased the people were with their church.

Plan and perspective of the Larkin Building, built in 1904. An example of a simple, utilitarian building with sheer brick walls and simple stone copings

Frank Lloyd Wright, 1910

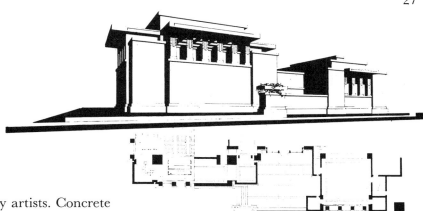

Drawing of Unity Temple—Oak Park,
Illinois, 1908. Concrete cast in
wooden forms with a textured surface
of bird's-eye gravel

Unity Temple was swept up by European architects and by artists. Concrete was liberated and instantly became a "new" material. Many painters of the time took merely the external effects of Unity Temple and modeled their theories of "cubism" on Frank Lloyd Wright's revolutionary use of form.

In 1906 Wright visited Japan. He found much of Japanese art and oriental philosophy akin to his own feeling. Their domestic architecture was more organic, he believed, than that of any other culture. Simplicity was their key —the spirit of their art. More than just the architecture of Japan, it was the Japanese print that he profoundly admired. The Japanese never imitated nature; they knew how to abstract natural forms subtly. Wright saw in this culture not an influence, but an affirmation of the very principles he believed in. From his first contact with Japan he began a collection of oriental art, which, despite tragic losses, is today one of the most extensive in the world.

* * *

In the autumn of 1909 the absorbing, intensive period of Frank Lloyd Wright's early architectural work came to a close. He was now forty. He had worked with fiery zeal, continuously, for more than ten years. Now he had unexpectedly reached a plateau in his work and in his nineteen years of marriage. He became restless in the home and family life. He then met, in his client Mamah Borthwick Cheney, an intelligent, cultivated woman and soon his appreciation of her turned into love. He asked his wife for a divorce, but she refused. The cataclysm of his situation was temporarily resolved when he was invited to spend some time abroad by the well-known German philosopher-critic Kuno Francke. He decided to go to Germany to work on the drawings for the forthcoming publication of his work—*Ausgeführte Bauten und Entwerfe* (*Executed Buildings and Drawings*). At the same time Henry Ford approached him concerning a building project. But with his sad and difficult family situation, he found it absolutely necessary to leave. As he had taken his destiny into his hands when he left home and college, so now he left his home and life in Oak Park. He sailed for Europe, and after a working sojourn in Berlin he lived in Fiesole, near Florence, Italy.

In 1911 he returned to the United States—his life in Oak Park now a finished epoch. The breaking up of his home, his work, and prestige in Oak Park was a painful experience which was the cause of much sorrow to himself and to all members of his family. But he believed that what he was doing was fundamentally right, and this faith carried him through. The architect returned to his ancestral valley to start again in work and life. His mother had given her son a wooded hill with a wide view of the Valley, knowing that at this precarious time he needed sanctuary. In this refuge the first Taliesin was built, and it stood not far from the tower Romeo and Juliet. Taliesin was the name of a Welsh bard who lived and recounted his legends of glory in the sixth century. Translated from the ancient Welsh it means "Shining Brow."

Chicago Architectural Photo Co.

Interior and section of Unity Temple
(also see page 110)

Dana house—early Wright design

Sandak

Chicago Architectural Photo Co.

Midway Gardens, 1913

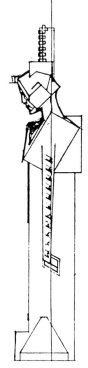

Pencil study of figure—later cast
for Midway Gardens

Detail of garden furniture—Midway Gardens

Like his grandfather before him, who had chosen America as the hope for a new life, the architect turned to this hill in the Valley for the beginning of his own. He built Taliesin as the brow upon that hill. Much of the house was constructed of yellow sand limestone found in neighboring quarries.

With life and work beginning again, he maintained a business office in Chicago's Auditorium Building, while the large working studio was at Taliesin. The months passed with increasing accomplishment. Designs and plans were drawn for structures that excited the imagination yet remained unbuilt. Even some of those erected were destroyed. In the autumn of 1913, Ed Waller commissioned the design for the Chicago Midway Gardens. Here the architect incorporated, in one vast scheme, indoor dining rooms, summer dining terraces, private dining rooms, an outdoor cabaret, and, for the first time, the outdoor orchestra shell. Every detail was designed by Frank Lloyd Wright: sculpture, paintings, murals, frescoes, furniture, linen, glass windows, spacious flower bowls and planting urns. Brick, with cast-concrete designs, formed decorative walls. Tall pinnacles of concrete-formed sculpture, now a machine craft under the direction of the architect, carried light standards up into the night sky from broad brick pedestals. Far ahead of its time, Midway Gardens was doomed by circumstances including Prohibition, and was torn down in 1923, existing today only in photographs and drawings. Here also Europe took inspiration, and the idea of geometric modern painting, called the "abstract" school, was taken from such murals as his "City by the Sea."

*   *   *

It was August of 1914, and architect Wright was just putting the finishing touches on Midway Gardens. He had spent the night, as he often did, at the gardens and was having his lunch there. But in the quiet summer noon an emergency telephone call from Spring Green reached him. The message was shocking. On his way home on the train he learned more of the tragedy from ghastly newspaper headlines: TALIESIN DESTROYED BY FIRE.

Thirty-six hours after Wright had left for Chicago, a Barbados negro who seemed a faultless servant had gone mad, setting fire to the house and taking the lives of seven people in the household, including Mrs. Cheney and her children. All the living quarters of the house were burned to the ground. But a faithful friend and some neighbors had saved the studios.

The architect came at dusk, and stood in the midst of destruction. In the unbelievable horror of this nightmare the master of Taliesin watched his life, his work, his love, smolder in the ashes. Where laughter and beauty had lived, there was nothing left now. No sound, no stirring of the air. The voices he had known and loved were gone. Great holes were burned into the black ashen ground. They were acrid, steaming from buried coals. Still black smoke hung over the hill in funeral wreaths. The devoted people who had loved him and served him were dead.

Time no longer existed. Somehow he lived through the following days. He tried to work, tried to salvage something from the ashes of his life. And everywhere over the ruin settled a terrible loneliness—an emptiness that destroyed whatever he tried to do. He left Taliesin and went back to his mother's house in Chicago. He grew ill. People turned to watch him uneasily as he passed them in the streets. But relatives, family and his children were kind and faithful to him. He was alone and needed help—but from where would help come? He could not endure life without work, so he started plans for the rebuilding of Taliesin.

Then, what seemed a miracle occurred in his life. In the autumn of 1914 an Imperial Commission from Japan came to Taliesin to invite him to design a great hotel for Tokyo. Through the Berlin publication by Wasmuth of Wright's early work, they discovered his name, now famous in Europe, and in turn had come to America. In Chicago they saw his architecture and sought him out at Taliesin. "We like your buildings very much, and although they are not Japanese in style, we nonetheless believe that you could build well for our country," they said. While still at Taliesin, Wright prepared some preliminary sketches for them to take to Tokyo. Shortly afterward came the invitation that he sail to Japan and begin work on the now world-famous Imperial Hotel.

Detail Imperial Hotel

* * *

The architect felt a deep sympathy with this ancient culture, and believed that any building designed for Japan must blend with it. Many European architects had forced Western styles upon the Japanese or had imitated Japanese architecture outright. Wright felt that both were sacrilege, and he sought to build with the feeling of the country and its traditions, without imitation. Where the industry and the machine of Western man could aid and teach the Japanese, he wished to show them a finer, safer way of constructing buildings.

The challenge of any building in Japan is the earthquake, which can sweep across the land at any moment in waves of violent destruction. Throughout its history, Japan had patiently rebuilt destroyed buildings. But the Imperial Hotel was to teach them how to live with the quake and survive it. To accomplish this aim, the architect spent months making studies of earthquakes and discovered that they behaved like waves of an ocean, rocking, swaying, and upheaving the earth in gigantic swells of motion. Careful studies of the build-

Detail, facade of Imperial Hotel

Imperial Hotel—Tokyo, Japan

Interior Imperial Hotel—Tokyo, Japan

Exterior, Imperial Hotel

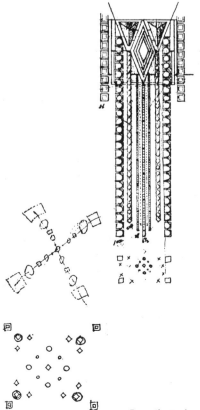

Pencil study of lighting fixture, Imperial Hotel

ing site revealed eight feet of spongy topsoil upon a substrata, sixty feet of mud. Just as the topsoil floated on a mud base, he believed that the building could also float upon that spongelike strata—with freedom to move with these waves of motion, resiliency would be a far safer solution than rigidity. Any attempt to withstand the quake in rigid forms would be destroyed. A building resting upon a network of tapering concrete pins piercing the top strata into the soft mud, and built upon the cantilever principle of reinforced-concrete slabs with the main support in the center, became the theory of the architect. Borings and tests were made and the system of "floating" the building proved sound. The centers of gravity, or heavier masses, were kept low to the ground. The walls were made of hollowed bricks, with concrete poured in between, forming a monolith with brick mosaic. The walls sloped inward as they rose. For decoration a lava stone called *oya* was found, which when wet from underground quarries was of the consistency of hard cheese and could be easily sculptured, but when in contact with the air hardened to become as light as green oak. These lava carvings were incorporated in the mosaic appliqué upon the reinforced-concrete slabs and walls. The customary heavy tiles of Japanese architecture treacherously slid off roofs and killed people during the tremor. On the Imperial Hotel the roof was made of light hand-worked copper. A huge pool for decoration and fire protection was designed to replace water systems which were usually destroyed during a quake.

Inside and out the architect designed every feature of the Imperial: rugs were woven for him in Peking, China; furniture, glassware, tableware, linen, window panes, sculpture, friezes, murals, and carved abstractions adorned this building. Electric coils in bathroom floors became his innovation of gravity heat. Private dining rooms, tea gardens, terraces, banquet hall, theater, along with the other component parts of a metropolitan hotel, made this building a famous meeting house for East and West.

In 1923 came the disaster that destroyed most of Tokyo—an earthquake that was the worst in the recorded history of man. Reports first said that the hotel had been destroyed, which he could not believe. He was in Los Angeles when he finally received a cablegram from a member of the Imperial family: "HOTEL STANDS UNDAMAGED AS MONUMENT OF YOUR GENIUS. HUNDREDS OF HOMELESS PROVIDED BY PERFECTLY MAINTAINED SERVICE. CONGRATULATIONS— BARON OKURA."

His genius not only saved the Imperial Hotel but gave refuge to multitudes of terrified people as they rushed up onto its terraces and into the sanctuary of the Imperial's protecting walls.

*   *   *

Several principles, without precedent in the field of architecture, combined to save the Imperial Hotel. Foremost among these was the cantilever: the extended floor or roof slab carried by a centered support. For centuries architects and engineers had relied upon the old post-and-beam construction. Essentially a wood type of construction, the ancient Greeks had carried this on into stone, disregarding the nature of the material. With the coming of steel, modern engineers progressed no further than the Greeks. They built with steel in a wood fashion, just as the Greeks built with stone in a wood fashion— ignoring the new freedom that this tensile product could offer. Of his conception of the cantilever, Frank Lloyd Wright said, "I concentrated on plasticity as physical continuity . . . it was inevitable that this esthetic ideal should be found to enter into the actual building of the building itself as a principle of construction. But I found that in the effort to actually eliminate the post and beam in favor of structural continuity, that is, making the two things now one instead of two separate things, I could get no help from regular engineers. By habit the engineer reduced everything in the field of calculation to the post and the beam resting upon it. Walls made one with floors and ceilings, merging together yet reacting upon each other, the engineer had never met . . . he had not enough scientific formulae to enable him to calculate for continuity. Floor slabs stiffened and extended as cantilevers over centered supports as a waiter's tray rests upon his upturned fingers, were new as I used them in the Imperial Hotel. . . ."

The post-and-beam type of construction is basically for building in wood technique: the vertical wooden support, with the horizontal joist, or beam, resting upon it and nailed to it. Throughout the history of architecture, buildings could frequently withstand pressure from without: the push or the thrust of wind or water. Weight and mass kept them rigid against these particular forces. But the idea of resisting horizontal forces by means of the continuity and flexible strength of steel in cantilevered concrete floors was entirely original with the Imperial Hotel. It was this continuity that saved the building from the earthquake. In the form of mesh, as thin wire, as flexible rods, the steel is also far more economical than the heavy girders and beams that were used in the steel-framed steel-skeleton buildings. A small steel member can easily do the work of a much larger wooden one.

*   *   *

During the completion stages of the Imperial Hotel, Aline Barnsdall commissioned a large residence for the top of Olive Hill in Los Angeles. California had taken the Spanish Mission style as its signature in architecture, but Frank Lloyd Wright began work on this house with the intention of giving this state an architecture native to her own character. Hollyhock House became the first poured-concrete house in America. Set on the crown of a high hill, in full sunlight the home protected its inhabitants from the hot sun by means of thick concrete walls but opened the rooms into small gardens and courtyards, reflection pools and shady lawns. Throughout the house the walls rose as concrete masses adorned with concrete sculptured abstractions on the motif of the client's favorite flower, the hollyhock.

In Japan the architect had become interested in another original form of building—the concrete block used as slab wall construction—and with his return to this country he put this new thesis into effect for Mrs. Alice Millard, of Pasadena. This was in 1924, at a time when the concrete block, like poured concrete before it, was considered a vulgar material. But he saw no reason why it could not have a beauty of its own. To this end he developed his "textile blocks": again, using the machine as a tool, each block was formed with an integrally impressed design. When put together in a wall or pier, linked by steel reinforcing rods and concrete poured into the joints to hold the steel to the block, the whole formed a monolithic patterned surface—strong and tensile. The separate blocks were single-surfaced, light, and easily manageable by workmen. La Miniatura was the pioneer in this new work, built in a small ravine bordered with eucalyptus trees, among foliage and plantings. The motif of the eucalyptus leaf became abstracted into the pattern of the block. As

Detail Millard house—Pasadena, California (also see page 112)

Taliesin in 1925

Japanese screen from the collection
of Frank Lloyd Wright

Japanese screen from the collection
of Frank Lloyd Wright

a pioneer presentation of a new system of structure, it underwent the usual trials of doubt on the part of contractors. Notwithstanding, Wright soon built other block houses as clients saw the beauty and integrity of this scheme.

Along with his houses in California, Frank Lloyd Wright over a period of seven years had been working on the Imperial Hotel, designs for three private homes, and a school, all in Tokyo. Sixteen times he crossed the Pacific, keeping in constant communication between these California houses and his projects in Japan. Meantime, the second Taliesin was being completed. He had collected many rare and beautiful works of art while in the Orient, some of which he built into the walls of Taliesin, and others—statuary, porcelain, bronze, screens, and prints—he placed throughout the house.

Having previously been granted a divorce from his first wife Catherine, he entered into a new and unsuccessful marriage with Miriam Noel, which after several years was dissolved.

*   *   *

Many young people from all over the world began coming to Taliesin. The fame of this beautiful, unique place had brought them to study and learn of its way of life. There were musical evenings when string quartets and fine soloists performed. The master especially loved Bach, Beethoven, and Handel. He read aloud to these young people from Walt Whitman, Emerson, Thoreau. As Taliesin was at work bringing the spirit of America to that small beginning group of scholars, so American artists and architects, vainly seeking culture beyond their own shores, were trying to graft the ways of Europe onto America.

But despite his accomplishments, the master of Taliesin was unhappy. Bitter memories of the past clung to the home he loved. He was, once more, alone.

*   *   *

It was the early spring of 1924. The architect had been staying in Chicago, and an artist friend invited him to a matinee performance of the ballet at Orchestra Hall. Frank Lloyd Wright, now in his middle fifties, was a strikingly handsome man. People looked at him with admiration. His aristocratic, leonine head was young and proudly held, his thick hair silvering around the temples.

The two men, having occupied a box in the loges, were waiting for the curtain to rise. The house lights started to dim, and as the performance was about to begin, the architect noticed a slender young woman being ushered into the box and showed to the one empty seat next to them. She was plainly dressed, with little make-up, and her long black hair was wound in a circlet around her head. She was very beautiful and reminded him of a Russian princess. His companion, the painter Jerry Bloom, also noticed her, and whispered that he remembered having met her at the house of a friend in New York. She was the daughter of the Chief Justice of the Supreme Court of Montenegro.

At intermission, Jerry Bloom introduced the young woman to Wright. She appeared reticent, and her voice had a lilting quality that distantly reminded the architect of the singing tones of the Welsh. He was impressed with her unusual beauty. When the painter praised the prima ballerina, the architect, turning to the young woman, remarked that the ballerina seemed dead —to him the whole experience was like watching the dead performing for the dead. At this comment the young woman glanced at him with keen interest. To her, also, the ballet had seemed lifeless. She told him that for many years she had devoted herself to the study of philosophy and had worked in music, dance, sculpture, and all the allied arts in Europe. From that moment the two became absorbed in a spirited conversation about philosophy and art, and although she had not heard of him, this distinguished man in turn deeply impressed her.

After the performance, when the two friends invited Olga Ivanovna to tea she accepted and asked them to call her Olgivanna—saying that in Tsarist Russia, where she had been educated, it was the custom to combine one's first name with the father's first name. They learned that she was married and had a seven-year-old daughter. But she had spent little time with her husband for the last several years. She spoke with a sadness in her voice that led the architect to believe that she was not happy in her marriage.

He left the next day for New York, and when he returned he called upon Olgivanna. Their previous meeting, brief as it had been, had impressed them both. They found themselves deeply in love and, after a courtship which held for each both happiness and sorrow, they were married. They spent many years of devoted life together.

* * *

Frank and Olgivanna Lloyd Wright began to build their life together at Taliesin in 1925. One cloudy evening as they were having supper in the detached dining-room quarters on the hilltop, they heard a storm rising. There was an intercom system throughout the house, and the phone buzzer in the little dining room began to ring incessantly. They grew worried as the storm became more violent, and left without finishing their meal. As they were coming down the steps from the hill to the main dwelling, they saw smoke rising from the master bedroom. There were only two people on the place besides themselves—the driver, Mell, and a Japanese apprentice, Kameki Tsachiurai. The architect called to them, and the three men rushed—too late —to the bedroom wing. Enormous flames had already burst and were pouring out of it. Because of a short in the intercom line, lightning had struck the house. Frantic calls for water were carried away in the steadily rising wind that fanned and fed the flames. "Fight the fire, fight—get water—fight it!" the

Allen Davison
Taliesin East today

Allen Davison
Wild Wisconsin roses, a favorite of Frank Lloyd Wright

Olgivanna Lloyd Wright, Taliesin, 1926

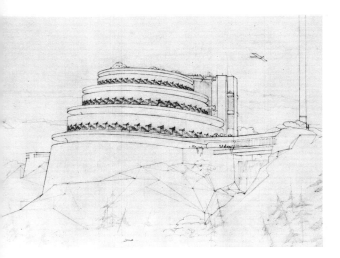

Gordon Strong Planetarium Project—
Sugarloaf Mountain, Maryland

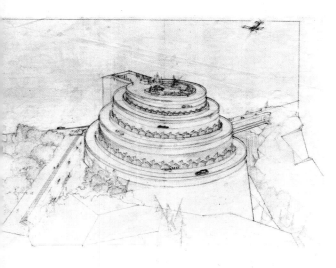

master shouted. Thunder crashed around them as the volume of the storm increased in fury. The fire—mounting and raging with every second—swept beneath the roof timbers and burst out from under the eaves. Wright climbed up onto the crackling roofs, fire searing his feet and his lungs. New currents of flame carried by the wind rolled onto the roof. "Frank—save yourself! Taliesin is gone!" Olgivanna called frantically. But he would not give up the fight. Many more men came to help—some running from their farms over the hills. And after a valiant fight of some twenty minutes the workrooms along with the drawings and sketches were miraculously saved.

Mercifully, the storm started to die. The lightning flashes faded, the wind changed its direction, and the rain came down. The studio had been spared, but again the living sections were a mass of charred stone and timber. And nearly every priceless work of art that had been in the house was gone. They searched in the ashes and were able to recover a few fragments and statues. He stood for a moment as he had eleven years before, but now Olgivanna stood by his side. "The real Taliesin stands wherever you are, Frank. Together we will build another Taliesin—even more beautiful than the one you have lost." And in the days succeeding the disaster, the little family lived in the house of the architect's sister Jane. Without waiting a day he went to work on drawings for the new Taliesin, now to arise once more out of the ashes of the old.

With two homes destroyed, with a large part of an invaluable collection of oriental art gone up in smoke, Wright was obliged to borrow money from the bank in order to rebuild. He had been commissioned to design several projects, and started those as soon as he could organize his studio. But although he had brought several working drawings to completion, they were not destined to be built in this time of grave need. His former wife, Miriam Noel, caused much trouble and was suing him for money and property. The architect's lawyer advised him to leave the vicinity for some three months, which, against his will, he finally decided to do. Olgivanna's health had been weakened—she was in serious need of rest and quiet. Her daughter by a former marriage, nine-year-old Svetlana, was living with them. They left Taliesin and drove to Minnesota, to find themselves still pursued by newspapers and legal difficulties. This continued for a long time until the pursuit was eventually called off. After having spent several months in Puerto Rico, New York, and La Jolla, the family was then able to return to Taliesin. Too much publicity had temporarily delayed his getting commissions. But his love for Olgivanna and hers for him was their greatest blessing and continued to uphold their strength and faith. Beauty was forever an important part of their life.

With his marriage to Olgivanna, there came a new epoch in the creative work of Frank Lloyd Wright. A series of sketches and plans were completed for the National Life Insurance Building in Chicago. Although this was never built, it was to be an important station in the architectural world, for it saw the birth of the skyscraper in a totally revolutionary sense. This project was called the Glass Skyscraper. No longer a steel-framed, concrete-coated rectangular box, as in the paved wilderness of American cities, the Glass Skyscraper rose in a triumph of light and air in flexible structure of concrete, glass, and sheet metal. The cantilever principle kept all supports for floors in the core of the building, while exterior walls, free from carrying weight, were transformed into screens of sheet copper and glass.

As new materials were being invented and perfected, architect Wright quickly discovered their organic characteristics. Now, with a still deeper understanding of the use and purpose of each new material, he perceived the endless possibilities of original forms. The old maxim that "form follows function" was to him outdated. That form and function must be one and the same in conception, structure, and design became a more useful and more beautiful solution. As is evident on New York's Park Avenue today, the acceptable construction up to this time had been to treat steel like lumber, built up in big post-and-beam constructions, faced with stone, wood, or brick—wasting the natural power of steel with its tension and tenuity, the capacity to be drawn to a fine thread and still remain strong. "Steel, like the spider spinning, should weave, pull and reinforce, thus entirely integral to its own nature." The Brooklyn Bridge of John Roebling is one fine example.

Striving for still more continuity, integrating structure and form, Wright explored another new field in 1925, when he made the drawings for the Gordon Strong Planetarium. Here was the circling ramp, where walls, ceilings, and floors became component parts of one another, their surfaces and forms flowing together as one consolidated whole.

For a noble building that would have the complete feeling and expression of steel, the architect drew his sketches for an all-steel cathedral in 1926. In the form of a many-sided pyramid, the vast structure was designed to hold many smaller chapels within, as a unity of the different faiths grouped together under one roof. From strong concrete masses at the base, steel beams rose along diagonal lines to meet at the apex. These beams were to be decorated with geometric designs also made of steel. The many-faceted roof surfaces were held by this network of beams, exposed to the outside to reveal their pattern and purpose. Had this cathedral been built then, it would have been the tallest structure in the world, designed to shelter 1,000,000 persons. But is was too far ahead of its time. The basic design idea of this cathedral was finally realized in the Beth Sholom Synagogue, built in 1959.

In 1927 more honors came for the architect from his building colleagues across the sea. Germany, Holland, and Japan published comprehensive monographs of his works. Still, no commissions were under construction. But he continued to expand the limits of the architectural world.

In the winter of the same year Wright and his family—Olgivanna, Svetlana, and their newly born daughter, Iovanna—went to Arizona, where he had been invited to work on a resort-hotel project, the Arizona Biltmore. With

North side of architect's camp "Ocotillo"
in the Arizona desert

Frank Lloyd Wright, 1930

about fifteen draftsmen working with him, he built a famous desert camp in the San Tan Mountains near Phoenix. It was called Ocotillo, the name of a desert plant with flamelike blossoms. This camp was constructed entirely of wood and canvas. Ten years later, again on the Arizona desert, the idea of textiles and plastics in architecture further evolved into the famous winter quarters of the Taliesin Fellowship—Taliesin West.

San Marcos on the desert, another challenge to conventional architecture, was projected in 1927 as a hotel resort near Chandler, Arizona. Concrete block, sheet metal, and glass were combined in outstretched terraces along the sides of two mountains. Experimental blocks were made and set up by Wright and his draftsmen, cast with patterns based on the triangle, a geometric form characteristic of the desert in that region. Destined to remain an unrealized project because of the nation-wide depression, it was nonetheless widely publicized and its influence among architects rapidly spread.

The unity of steel and concrete gave the architect boundless artistic freedom. With the elimination of post-and-beam construction came this plasticity which Frank Lloyd Wright had felt and begun in his early Prairie Houses; but now, through his entirely original use of the cantilever, he was able continually to expand this principle. These projects also brought another unit into focus—the diamond module with the 60°–30° triangle, both in plan and in elevation. Ordinary rigid shapes were giving way to more plastic, fluent expressions of form.

All aspects of life and living came into Frank Lloyd Wright's ever widening scope of vision. A simple gas station was made into a beautiful circumstance of cantilevered construction and decorative steel suspension cables. It remained a project on paper until it was built in 1956 in Minnesota.

In 1929 Wright drew plans for St. Mark's Tower in New York City. Here he again innovated a remarkable idea for skyscraper construction. A cross-shaped reinforced-concrete pylon extends the full height of the tower from foundation to roof terrace above. This cross form divided each floor level into four apartments—and supported their cantilevered slabs as well. By means of a polygonal plan the rooms have an abundance of light and air, with small balconies and projecting terraces. The following year he evolved this same scheme into a connected group of apartment towers for Chicago. In 1940, this idea was developed in the Crystal Heights Hotel for Washington, D.C. Here the towers were of different heights, all rising like a group of spires from long terraces below that would contain shopping centers, theaters, and parks. None of these was built. In 1956, the H. C. Price Company commissioned a tower for Bartlesville, Oklahoma, the realization of the basic St. Mark's scheme.

The years just before the founding of the Fellowship, a school for architects, were devoted family years for the architect. However financially limited, they lived in a home that they themselves had created and made beautiful. A favorite excursion was to rise at dawn—all four walking barefoot down to the watermelon patch with their dog, Kavey. The white mornings in early autumn were cold and the ground covered with hoarfrost. There in the frosty dew they would split the melons across their knees and make their breakfast of the luscious rose-colored fruit that lay in ripe abundance throughout the garden. How they loved the tall, spired grasses that shone with rainbow spheres of dew.

Spiders wove their webs meshed with those cool, slender drops. Delicately hung, the webs spanned flowers and leaves like fine threads of glass and thin steel strands.

The rich days passed in the continuous motion of happiness, creation, and work. Wright spent much time with his children and devised games with blocks that could form intriguing, imaginative patterns. He loved to play the piano, always improvising. All day long music could be heard in the house; if not being rehearsed by some family member, it was played on records, which he listened to for hours on end. He and Olgivanna with their two daughters went on long walks through the Valley gathering branches along country roadsides and high up in the hills.

The architect and his wife were accomplished in many diverse ways. Often in the early mornings before breakfast they worked together on some of the rhythmic patterns of the dances Olgivanna had studied abroad. In the evenings they read aloud to each other or would often discuss art, medicine, religion, their plans for starting the Fellowship. In winter they skated on the frozen ponds below the house. With a practiced eye in the beauty of motion, Olgivanna enjoyed watching his tigerlike grace as he glided freely over the silvery, mirror-smooth surface.

The years passed with swift momentum, and the world was becoming more aware of the life and work at Taliesin. Greater honors came to the architect. He gave many exhibitions of his work across the country, and universities invited him to lecture. He delivered a series of talks at Princeton in 1930, and in 1931 another series at the Chicago Art Institute. Princeton University compiled these lectures into a book called *Modern Architecture,* and the Chicago Art Institute published a large pamphlet with photographs.

John Amarantides

Bottlebrush, Arizona flower

In 1930 he sailed with Mrs. Wright to Rio de Janeiro. The National Academy of Brazil had invited him to judge a competition for a memorial to Christopher Columbus. They were greeted with tremendous enthusiastic receptions there, and he returned to the United States with citations of honor conferred by the Belles Artes Academy of Brazil.

Shortly after, he worked out a plan for the Chicago World's Fair of 1933. He had rejected proposals to design a few separate buildings, and instead presented his concept for the fair as a whole. He designed three schemes, including skyscraper, suspension bridges, and floating barges. When the fair ended, these buildings could be used by the city for industry, offices, and entertainment. This project remained unbuilt. Instead, the fair was done as a baroque classical revival, complete with nymphs.

Prefabricated apartments, 1915

Horizon Press

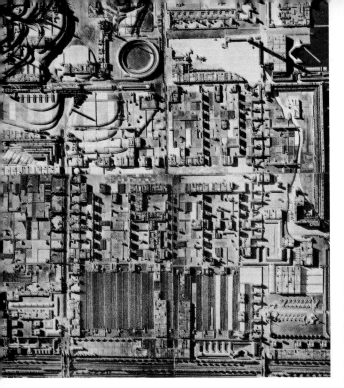

Photograph of Broadacre City model

Hundreds of varieties of cactus, desert trees, and wild flowers grow in the foothills of the McDowell Mountains, location of Taliesin West

Allen Davison

Through the lean years of the early thirties, when the building industry was almost at a standstill in the United States, Frank Lloyd Wright devoted his time to a unique thesis which he called Broadacre City. Based on the idea that each person should have at least an acre of ground allotted to him, Wright envisioned a green countryside interspersed with buildings. Towers rose among lush planting and foliage. Highways and industries were surrounded by sweeping wooded parks. He planned highway systems complete with specially designed bridges, railroad track intersections, highway routes laid out for trucks and large vehicles to keep them out of the main arteries of traffic. Amusement centers and huge markets flanked hillsides; dwellings and business centers were formed over hills and prairies.

Each home was designed for the minimum land unit of one acre. With standard units of sheet metal, the architect worked out a plan for a little country house and farm buildings that could be easily assembled and expanded as needed. The idea of prefabricated housing was his innovation, which he first presented in 1915 with the "American System Ready-Cut" prefabricated apartments. Wright saw our present-day city as an outmoded way of life. With the vastly rising population and the countless vehicles of the machine age, man could no longer afford to press and crowd with his neighbors, as he had into the twentieth century. The architect knew that the old city was vanishing. This idea came at a time when almost no thought of decentralization had entered the mind of the nation. In 1934, as a project, the Taliesin Fellowship built Broadacre City into a comprehensive model. Wright wrote and published a book describing it called *The Disappearing City*.

"In Roman times the city was a normal instrument—indispensable means of communication from the outside, at once a meeting place and a cultural center. Now it is merely a hangover habit—mankind's mediocrity and lack of imagination. The lower instincts of humanity began to take their course. The gregarious animal nature never builds up—only levels down. The herd has never been the proper place for culture."

* * *

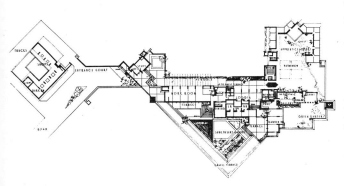

Early plan of Taliesin West

In 1932 the architect and his wife founded the Taliesin Fellowship at their home near Spring Green, Wisconsin. They began by training a few young men and women, some of whom stayed on as faculty members. During twenty-eight years of its operation, over a thousand young people have come from all over the world to study architecture and culture according to organic principles. The early years of the Fellowship were difficult but challenging, and made increasing demands upon its two founders. They believed that young people should learn many different kinds of work and should master architecture in its manifold forms. The hardships of those beginning years were picturesque and full of adventure. In Wisconsin, even with the cold winter temperature below zero, construction work went on as part of the students' training.

Taliesin West, general view

Mr. and Mrs. Wright decided that it would benefit the student-apprentices to make changes in their environment. In 1938 they went to Arizona and bought land in the desert, twenty-five miles northeast of Phoenix. Here they decided to build and establish a new Taliesin where the student-apprentices would spend the winter months of each year. The site they chose was a gradual slope against the foothills of the McDowell Mountains overlooking Paradise Valley. It is mountainous country, full of richly colored volcanic stone. There are broad plains and valleys of dry clay and airy vegetation which become fertile and green with the rains. In the years that followed, the whole Fellowship—some seventy-five young people—moved from Taliesin in Wisconsin to the desert camp each November, remaining until May first, then returning north again.

*   *   *

For Taliesin West, Wright conceived a building that expressed the spirit of the mountains—with mesa-like terraces, broad steps bringing one level into another like merging plateaus, and a triangular prow extending into the desert and its view on the southwest. From the abundance of volcanic rock he developed a new thesis in masonry construction. The student-apprentices hauled stone from surrounding terrain, dug sand from the washes for making concrete. Using temporary wooden forms, these stones are held together by the concrete, with their flat surfaces exposed. A stone mosaic is built up in the various walls. Huge redwood beams are the superstructure, with panels of clear white canvas set between them, giving a soft translucent light inside.

Interior Taliesin West

With the laying of the first foundations of Taliesin West in 1938, the architect and his family lived in tents as did all Fellowship members. Work was carried on in spite of fierce driving rains, lashing winds, and dust storms. Meals were cooked in a wood-and-canvas lean-to—a temporary construction in a rocky ravine. Taliesin West was built entirely by the student-apprentices under the architect's direction.

Olgivanna Lloyd Wright

Mrs. Wright describes the buildings and development of Taliesin West in her book, entitled *The Shining Brow—Frank Lloyd Wright:* "When we started build- ing the camp in the Arizona desert, Mr. Wright used only stone, redwood and canvas, because the climate was mellow and sunny with very little dampness or rain. But the climate began to grow more severe in the ensuing years and I believed that we should replace the canvas with glass. He did not like to relinquish the idea of a building made of stone, wood and textiles. 'But the weather has changed—there are too many cold days, and even the rainy days have increased. This prevents us from opening the canvas flaps and has been forcing us into the use of too much artificial light,' I pleaded. 'You are the only one in the whole world who will know how to combine glass and canvas. Please put the glass in so we can always see the beauty of the mountains.'

"But he still wanted to believe that the Arizona climate would change back to what it was thirty years before.

"Seven years went by, and one morning I woke up under the fresh impression of a dream. 'I dreamed,' I told him, 'that you had built a long room extending

Apprentices working on
a building at Taliesin West

Allen Davison

from the Sun Terrace to the Point. The two walls were of solid stone, the other two were huge sheets of glass interrupted by stone piers in long intervals. There was a glittering storm in the desert—the lightning streaked over Camel-back Mountain, the wind whirled the clouds, McDowell Range was blue. Diagonal lines of rain slashed its sides. You and I were standing together watching and enjoying the storm.'

"He smiled very gently. 'All right, Mother, we will use glass with the canvas.'

" 'But it is the truth,' I exclaimed. 'I did have this dream last night.' But by then he and the boys were already taking measurements for the glass. And of course he was the only one who could have combined these two materials with such perfect harmony. There was little need to change the lines of the structure. The camp turned into a transparent phantom desert ship with ever-moving colors of the plains and mountains. The remaining canvas flaps have to be replaced every three years; those less exposed to the sun every five or six years. That is easily done, because the frames are removable; our apprentices simply stretch new canvas on frames."

*　　*　　*

The most published residence by Frank Lloyd Wright was his home for E. J. Kaufmann, Fallingwater, completed in 1937. Here for the first time he used the reinforced-concrete cantilever in residential architecture. The architect said that he was jealous of the wide publicity given to this house; because when asked what he considered his greatest masterpiece, he inevitably replied, "The next one."

This house is an abstraction of the spectacular site: a steep wooded slope in a forest glade, studded with outcropping rock, large boulders, and looking down upon a rushing stream that falls in cascades making pools on different levels. When the architect first visited the site in Bear Run, Pennsylvania, he noticed a boulder nestled against the side of the hills a few yards above the stream. "Here will be the hearth for the fireplace, and the broad chimney tower will rest on this large stone. All other rooms and levels will be related to it."

After returning to Taliesin he drew a magnificent plan. Various rock outcrop-pings were used as design-structure features. Stone piers and walls built directly out of the rock bed of the rushing stream hold wide cantilevers. A great living room is carried by these piers from the projecting rock against the side of the hill, out past the limbs of trees, and over the rushing falls with surfaces of smooth concrete and stratified stone. Deep-toned polished walnut is fash-ioned into generous bookshelves, ledges, and low, wide tables. Rugs of oriental fabrics, furs, and skins spread on stone-paved floors make a rich interior. Small balconies and broad roof terraces open the rooms at different levels to hillside views of trees, rhododendron, and mountain laurel—even to the sounds of birds and rushing water. This house is a poem of spaciousness within itself and lives in close harmony with the spirit of the earth.

He often spoke of the cantilever as evident in a tree. Yet he would never copy the form of a tree. He understood the principle of structure from the roots anchored in the earth, growing into the trunk, the branches continuing this growth movement. Then the more delicate limbs that sweep out from the branches and into patterns of leaves. The tree breathes and absorbs sunlight through this final integrated ornament of nature.

MACHINERY

RESEARCH

DEVELOPMENT

HEIGHT ABOVE
GROUND–153 FT.
15 FLOORS

QUALITY
CONTROL

LIBRARY

GROUND LEVEL

BASEMENT

CONCRETE CORE 54 FEET DEEP

Section diagram of the
Johnson Wax Tower, 1950

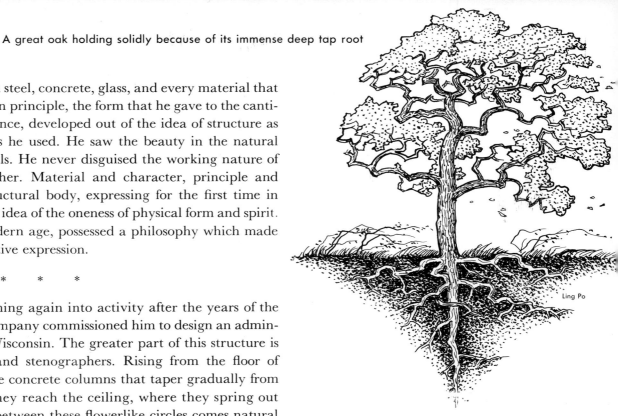

Ling Po

S. C. Johnson & Son, Inc.

He used this same principle with steel, concrete, glass, and every material that came into his scope of creation. In principle, the form that he gave to the cantilever, its character and appearance, developed out of the idea of structure as an organic part of the materials he used. He saw the beauty in the natural qualities of all building materials. He never disguised the working nature of one material to resemble another. Material and character, principle and design, were fused into one structural body, expressing for the first time in modern architecture the timeless idea of the oneness of physical form and spirit. Wright, the architect of the modern age, possessed a philosophy which made of his work and his life one creative expression.

* * *

With the building industry coming again into activity after the years of the depression, the Johnson Wax Company commissioned him to design an administration building for Racine, Wisconsin. The greater part of this structure is a large workroom for typists and stenographers. Rising from the floor of the main room are slender white concrete columns that taper gradually from nine inches at the base until they reach the ceiling, where they spring out into eighteen-foot disks. Down between these flowerlike circles comes natural light for the room through patterned glass-tube skylights.

The Wisconsin Building Commission demanded that the strength of the columns be tested. These slender shafts, required to carry twelve tons of weight to support the building, were unheard of in the building codes, which stated that a column with a nine-inch base could be no higher than six feet. The dendriform shafts, increasing in diameter as they rose, were twenty-four feet high. A test column was constructed with steel-mesh reinforcements, a steel shell embedded in the outer concrete flesh of the shaft: the circular membrane of steel thus becoming one with the flesh or coating of concrete.

A public field test was arranged. With a steam shovel, loads of weighed gravel and cement bags were piled on the flat disk top of one column. All day long gathering crowds, roped off from the site by police, watched and waited as sixty tons of gravel and cement were loaded onto this incredible column. Delicate-looking as a white stem, it withstood the piling weight until finally at sunset it had to be pulled down. As it fell to the ground nothing but the top disk broke—the column itself had remained intact.

Upon completion the story of the Johnson Wax Building was immediately published in magazines throughout the world. Thousands of visitors and admirers came from near and far, as they do today.

* * *

Architect Wright wanted to give to America an economically priced home of its own that would also be a work of art. In 1937 he designed the first Usonia home in Madison, Wisconsin. In this home the natural floor heating formed by hot-water pipes set beneath a concrete floor was first used in America and soon became current architectural practice. The chimney mass and bearing walls that carry the roof are made of red brick. The other walls throughout the house, inside and out, are another invention of the architect. A core of plywood is faced on each side with insulation, then surfaced with cypress boards. These laminated walls can be constructed on the ground, raised in place as one unit, and assembled like a prefabricated house.

Johnson Wax Administration Building
showing controversial columns

Rendering of Monona Terrace at night

42

Mr. and Mrs. Wright in 1938

Jacobs house—Wisconsin, 1938

Monona Terrace from the lake

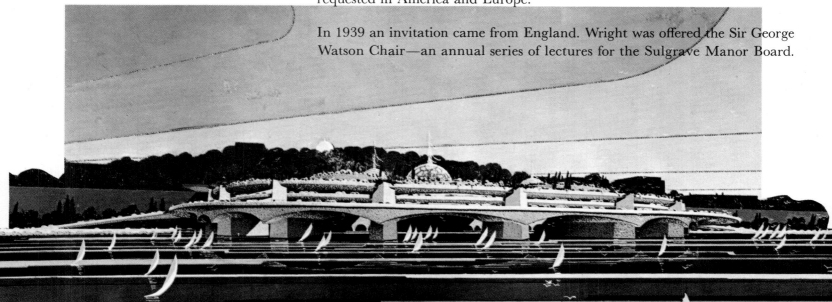

This simple but revolutionary structure became the forerunner for dozens of smaller homes built by the architect all over America during the next ten-year period. He used and continued to develop the unit system, on which the homes were built applying ever new geometric shapes in basic plan. The Hanna house was the first residence built using the unit system of the hexagon, the six-sided equilateral figure like the honeycomb. Architect Wright felt that the hexagon was flexible, and from this unit he soon developed the ultimate of flexibility—the circle.

From 1938 onward, the circle was used more frequently by him in his work. In 1939 he designed the Monona Terrace Civic Center for Madison, Wisconsin, using large arcs and patterns of different-sized circles. But contractors were not accustomed to this form. They had to be taught the means of handling it. No units of standardization in industry had considered it. Gradually his pioneer work in this field caught on and was used by others in the field of architecture.

* * *

American colleges had always been built as imitations of traditional European buildings. Wright saw this as an impediment to the growth of our own culture. Just as a home should serve the needs of man in both the domestic and spiritual senses, so a college should have an architectural significance, in its service as an educational building and as an inspiration to the students and faculty alike.

With the courage and perseverance of President Ludd M. Spivey, of Florida Southern College, the architect drew up extensive plans in 1938 for a sixteen-building campus. This was the first time in America that a college was designed as integral to site, purpose, and time. The campus is situated on the shores of a lake in the heart of Florida. A warm winter climate made more open planning possible. With concrete block, poured concrete, steel, and glass, an architectural grammar was created that would give unity to the campus as a whole. Over a period of years, as funds became available, various buildings were erected. By means of a continuous esplanade, each of the buildings is connected to the other. It stands today as a prophetic reality of what architecture can be when it grows out of the roots of principle.

* * *

Along with this prodigious output of his creative work, he found time to lecture and write. Continually called upon by universities and colleges to speak to students, he clearly defined his ideas and inspired them to look into the meaning and significance of architecture. Many exhibitions of his work were requested in America and Europe.

In 1939 an invitation came from England. Wright was offered the Sir George Watson Chair—an annual series of lectures for the Sulgrave Manor Board.

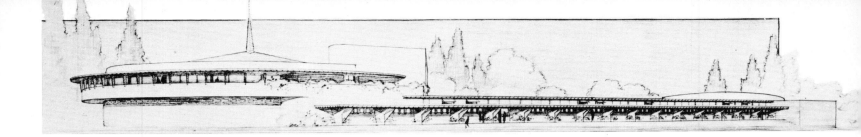

In the spring of that year, accompanied by his wife and daughter, he traveled to London, where he delivered these lectures. They were later published under the title *An Organic Architecture*. He spoke to packed halls everywhere; many hundreds were so eager to hear him that crowds of people had to be turned away. The Royal Institute of British Architects honored him with their Gold Medal; in 1941 he also received, among King George's birthday honors, the Royal Gold Medal for Architecture. For two years after his return to the United States his architectural activity went on as always until America entered the Second World War. American building except for that of the war effort came to a halt.

During the war years, although no actual work was under way, the architect's creative output continued. Among several proposed projects was one for the Government, the Cloverleaf-quadruple housing project: one hundred houses for a hundred-acre tract, near Pittsfield, Massachusetts.

Architect Wright was still working on the simple inexpensive type of home. He made his first design for a berm type of house in 1942. Berm construction uses earth banked up against the outside walls of the building. This is excellent insulation against both heat and cold, and reduces cost. For a group of co-operative homesteads for Detroit auto workers, the architect devised a small plan with the earth graded up to the level of the window sills, and then spread out as low embankments away from the house. These banks were to be planted with grasses and clover.

Florida Southern University

Frank Lloyd Wright was now growing into his seventies and into one of his most productive periods. Completely absorbed in each project, however great or small, he worked out its minutest details, watched over each step taken by the members of his staff and their rendering of his sketches, consulted client and contractors to see his plan fully realized in its utmost perfection.

At this time Solomon R. Guggenheim was planning to build a museum in New York City to house a large number of modern paintings. Wright was asked if he would take the job and if he would submit some sketches. Thus began one of the greatest artistic achievements of all time.

Herbert A. Jacobs

Herbert A. Jacobs house—
Middleton, Wisconsin, 1942
Berm type construction

When the design of the Guggenheim Museum was made public every obstacle was thrown in the way of its completion. The building commissioners of New York City had never seen anything like it. They tried cutting it down to their own codes and insisted upon making changes. The spiral form confused them, and because there were no separate floors in the museum, they tried to condemn it as not fireproof. Mr. Guggenheim waited for building prices to go down before beginning construction and instead the prices skyrocketed. Because of its totally original idea, many doubted and distrusted it. After sixteen years of struggle, during which architect Wright fought unceasingly for his building, he won.

His principle of continuity reached unparalleled beauty with the ramp and circle combined in this building as an ever ascending spiral. Steel mesh,

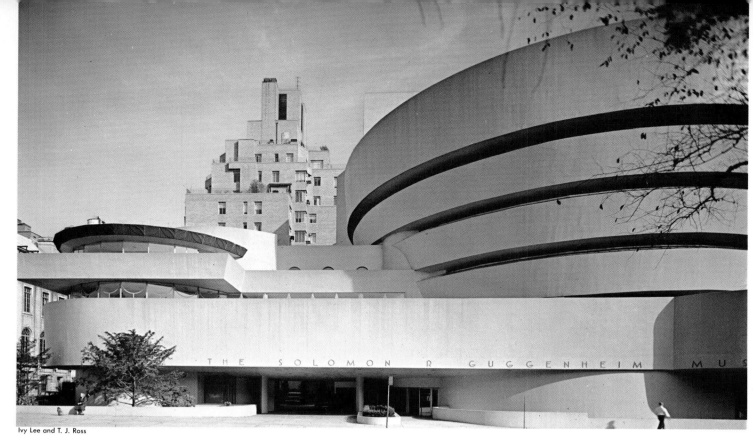

Ivy Lee and T. J. Ross

Guggenheim Museum

Model of Guggenheim Museum

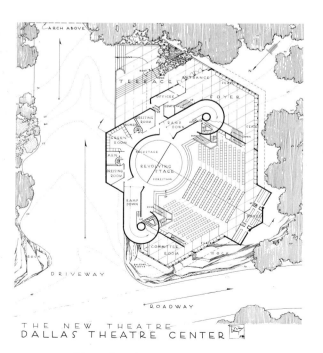

THE NEW THEATRE
DALLAS THEATRE CENTER

Plan of Dallas Theater

embedded in the concrete, was like the tendons beneath the flesh of the human body. With its plasticity, concrete could be molded into any desired form. Steel, with its miraculous quality of being able to pull, was the strengthening fiber. The Guggenheim Museum has awakened a sense of the possibilities for spiritual beauty within a building. It has become a central meeting point for all students and lovers of art throughout the world.

Frank Lloyd Wright stands today as the greatest form giver in the history of architecture. With the Prairie Homes he gave America an architecture of her own. With the Guggenheim Museum and many other buildings of equal stature he became a prophet hundreds of years ahead of his time.

Also in the same year he designed a house to be built for V. C. Morris on the ocean coast near San Francisco. Rising dramatically from the surf, the house would be constructed of earthquake-proof reinforced concrete growing out of the cliff itself. Slender tapering semi-tubular forms rise from the sea, gradually becoming larger until they support the main living part of the house at the top of the cliff. A stately entrance, planted with flowers and vines, approaches the house and its ocean view. Over the windows of the living room reaches a great visor of waterproof concrete, designed to be topped with soil and planted, framing a broad view of the sea through hanging vines and shade-giving foliage. Mr. and Mrs. Morris were in love with their house on the cliff, but they died before they could fulfill their dream. (*See page 121.*)

When the Unitarian Society of Madison asked Wright to design a church for them he searched for a new pattern that would create an ideal atmosphere to worship in. He discussed this problem with his wife and she suggested that he design the church in the form of a triangle. The preacher would stand at the apex and thus all the congregation would be focused toward him. The roof should symbolize the gesture of hands in prayer, expressing warmth and love. With a characteristic swiftness of imagination, Wright produced one of his most beautiful designs. The basic plan of the church became a triangle, crowned by a triangular copper roof—"the gesture of hands in prayer."

Mrs. Wright was an impartial judge of her husband's work. He trusted her strong sense of proportion, her judgment of color and form. He often called her into the drafting room to ask her what she thought of some new scheme. Years of this work together instilled in her an exceptional sense of form in architecture and endowed her with the force to carry on the execution of his work.

Sensitivity to the problems of acoustics and seating arrangement came naturally to Wright. He had a vivid feeling for drama. In 1955 he was asked to build a new theater for Dallas, Texas. Thus came the perfected form of the architect's long consideration of the theater. Seating is designed to go half way around a circular stage. Vision and acoustics are uniformly excellent from every seat in the house. The stage itself is a revolving circle, affording infinite possibilities for theatrical productions. Lighting comes from a balcony that surrounds the theater and also descends from the ceiling and from the sides. The New Theatre is designed to bring about more connection between actor and audience and is creating a fresh medium of dramatic presentation.

*   *   *

While the members of his staff were completing the drawings for the Greek Orthodox church in Milwaukee, Wisconsin, the architect was creating the most important idea for tall-building construction in the world of architecture. This was the skyscraper called the "Mile-High Sky City Illinois," designed to be five times higher than the tallest existing structure in the world, the Empire State Building. The framework of the Illinois is in principle like a tree; the horizontal floor slabs extend from the vertical core, making the total structure light and strong.

Huntington Hartford Country Club

Unitarian Church from the prow—Madison, Wisconsin
Ezra Stoller

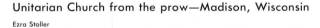

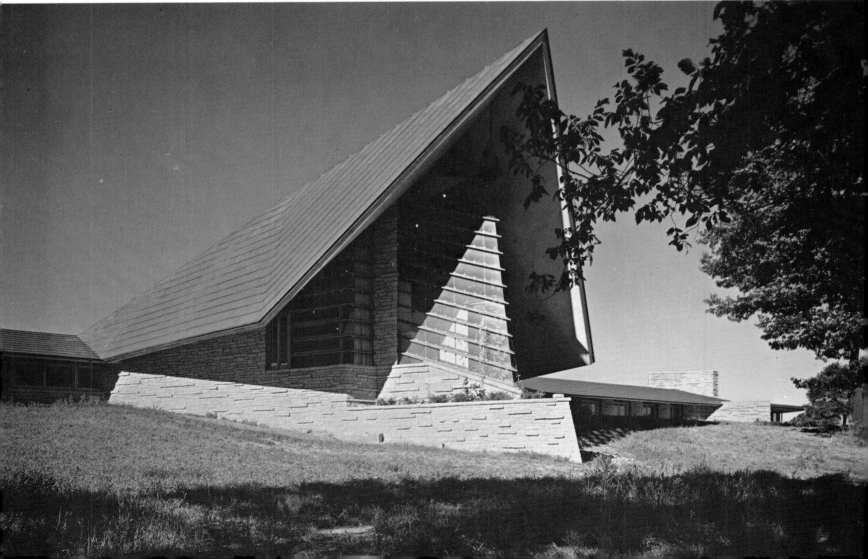

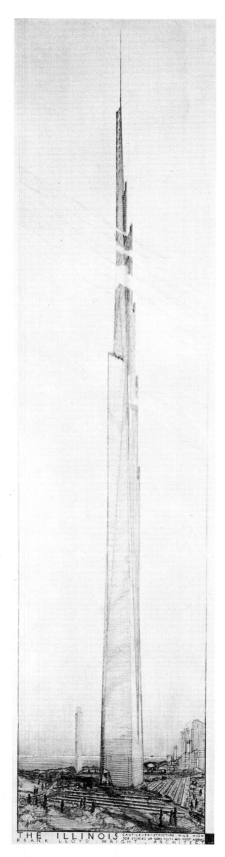

Mile High Sky City Project—
Chicago, Illinois, 1956

There are 528 floors, made hollow in the center for space in which to hold air-conditioning, lighting, and heating systems. All the glass surfaces outside are set back beneath a metal visor for sun protection. The Illinois again uses the taproot foundation as in the Johnson Tower and the Price Tower. This spine reaches far down into bedrock to give the structure solidity at extreme heights. With a stable central core and suspension cables the building would be supple yet firm enough to withstand violent winds. This pioneering structural concept is a tapering form that soars into the sky like a saber of glass and steel, its handle sunk deep into the earth.

The overcrowded cities such as New York and Chicago would no longer be necessary. The man working in the Illinois could live in a free spacious countryside and drive to his place of work through green terrain, leaving his car on one of the broad parking terraces which reach out at the base of Sky City.

*　　*　　*

For the Marin County Government Center he created a building of reinforced concrete that connects three hilltops and spans the valleys between them, incorporating all county administrations in a lovely pastoral landscape. The idea of decentralizing government buildings, bringing them out into the countryside, is now being realized in this project as it was first stated in *The Disappearing City. (See page 120.)*

The Oasis was Frank Lloyd Wright's design in 1957 for a new state capitol to be built near Phoenix, Arizona. The site he suggested was at the foot of red granite mountains in a state park. Colonnades of onyx support a lattice dome of concrete beams. Beneath this arbor in patterned sunlight are gardens and pools, walks paved with mosaic tiles, shaded and cool. Space within is provided for exhibitions and seating capacity. Rising out of the sides of the dome are two large chambers, the Senate and the House of Representatives. Two wings extending into gardens contain other government offices. This was the architect's vision of an organic building suited to the terrain. It was refused by the state in their preference for a building that could stand on any avenue of New York City. Yet the plans for the Oasis record a landmark of newborn ideas.

Frank Lloyd Wright was invited in the spring of 1957 to Baghdad, Iraq. The government asked him to design an opera house, post office, and cultural center. He had long admired the Persian and Sumerian cultures; their national heritage—Biblical and Moslem—inspired his imagination. The opera house was designed as a large circular building set inside a park and surrounded by parking levels forming a wide circle and approached by ramps. The domelike roof was to be held by two steel crescents which emerge from the outside of the buildings to rise and meet inside and form the proscenium arch over the stage. In these lattice crescents were to be set large bronze medallions showing various legends of the *Arabian Nights.* At the base of the crescents tiers of water rise and splash in different levels into green gardens. A metal lattice dome on the roof of the opera house was to contain a sculptured abstraction of Aladdin's lamp. According to Biblical tradition, this land of the Tigris and Euphrates is the cradle of civilization, and the architect envisioned a building in a garden park on a small island in the Tigris River. Sculptures of Adam and Eve in the center would be surrounded with stone figures representing the various races —all set among fruit trees. A gallery, art museum, and bazaar kiosks were also planned for this extensive Baghdad project. For the heart of the city itself he designed a post-office building. But a sudden upheaval and revolution in Iraq halted the realization of these buildings.

* * *

When the Beth Sholom Congregation, of Elkins Park, near Philadelphia, asked Frank Lloyd Wright to design them a synagogue, he gave detailed study to the Jewish faith, its history and symbols. Mrs. Wright said in her address at the dedication of the synagogue: ". . . Then in this somber twentieth century of ours there arose an architect—a man who daringly built a synagogue through which the voices of God and Moses were called again to life in visible form. The spirit of Mount Sinai grew on a street, independent, strong, declaring its original faith when man spoke directly to God and God answered man. Their voices ring through sheets of glass and plastic, through steel and concrete, through living forms of today, binding them with the power of their noble past to seal their legacy to the future. The white light like the breath of God pours through the walls and descends from the high pyramidal dome embracing the Torah, the eternal light; the Menorahs, the voice of the cantor, the rabbi, and the throbbing silence of the congregation.

"Rare among men, this creator of new forms, when he designed and built, gave to each religious faith its own symbol. This synagogue is the symbol of victory over the destructive forces and the persecution of the Jewish faith. It is a new architectural expression whose roots are dipped into the long measures of Time—and which has once more risen in the proud dignity and character of its faith. The temple fulfills the indestructible wish of the human soul to share in divine beauty and to feel the presence of God. . . ."

A few weeks before his death on April 9, 1959, he designed for Arizona State University a fine-arts center. This included an auditorium, recital hall, and classrooms for their drama and art departments. When this is constructed, it will be the first public building by Frank Lloyd Wright to be built in the state of Arizona, where he lived for much of his lifetime.

Also in April of 1959, Wright designed the Donahoe Triptych. It will be built upon three separate peaks that form the top of a small mountain rising out of the Arizona desert. A road winds up between the peaks and under sweeping arches of masonry bridges. These arched bridges connect the houses on each peak. The Triptych becomes the crown of the mountaintop, growing out of it in native desert materials.

* * *

During his phenomenally productive lifetime Frank Lloyd Wright created hundreds of other designs and buildings which are not included in this biography. He also wrote many books about his life and work.

His last design was the drawing for a walled garden at Taliesin in Wisconsin. It was intended for Mrs. Wright as a beautiful retreat from their constantly active life. The garden is set into a slope of the hill on which Taliesin is built, and is rectangular in form with high walls to the west and north. One side opens onto a romantic view of the valley, hills, and the tower Romeo and Juliet. These walls are built of the same sand limestone used throughout the house and in bright sun they are of a soft golden hue. Two large round entrances open into the garden, and set into these circles are red-and-gold doors of wood and bronze. Semicircular steps lead from these moon gates to the interior

Auditorium for
Arizona State University 1959

Guerrero

Temple Beth Sholom (also see page 103)

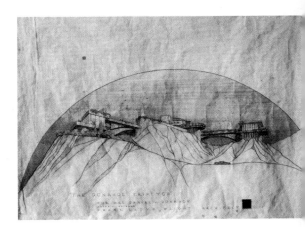

Donahoe Triptych

of the garden. Out of a round aquamarine-blue pool rises a fountain disk made of patterned red metal, upon which the fountain jet splashes with a softly ringing sound. Statues and Ming porcelain adorn the walls and on the edge of the pool float multicolored glass spheres. The students did the stonemasonry and brought many luxuriant plants, which Mrs. Wright has placed throughout her garden. On the lawn are tables of metal and glass, garden chairs, and circular sunshades of turquoise-and-white fabric, designed by Mrs. Wright and made at Taliesin. A hundred rose bushes, petunias, geraniums, marigolds, and phloxes embroider the garden walls. Guests, faculty members, and students are often invited for refreshments or dinners in Mrs. Wright's rose garden.

* * *

Far beyond the age when most men retire from their professions or rest upon past achievements, Frank Lloyd Wright grew with a sustained force. In his eighties his supreme imagination continued to discover new and changing forms. Until his very last few days on earth, his life was devoted to work and to creation.

Whenever Wright was not directing or designing in the drafting room, he was continuously engaged in a different kind of activity. He would often study the fields where the grains made patterns on the landscape as he had laid them out. There was not a square of earth that escaped his constantly alert, creative eye. He had planned the fields, trees, contours of pastures—even to the animals on the farm. He loved the way brown Guernsey cows looked silhouetted against Wisconsin hillsides. He made lakes and ponds out of the old creek beds and worked ceaseless hours standing in the cold mud, walking back and forth, pointing and marking the land with his cane, telling just where the steam shovel should dig out the ground. He not only directed the making of roads on Foundation land but would himself ride the road grader, turning the big wheels of the heavy-bladed machine as the tractor lurched over the stones. He knew rest only by changing his work. If he grew tired at the drafting board, writing, or working outside, he would arrange foliage in the house or place beautiful works of art—vases, sculpture, statues, flowers, prints, furnishings—until they formed such harmonious patterns that "you could play them like a beautiful melody."

Without hesitation he would make any change he thought was needed at Taliesin. Often as he and Olgivanna went out walking, contemplating the buildings, he would call to a group of students working near by, "Boys, bring the crowbar—we're going to change this wall!" And as they tore down the stone or concrete and steel and glass, he was giving directions for the building of the new one.

* * *

With his resolute insight and his direct, incisive wit, he could take his enemies apart and expose the things he did not believe in. But he never hated anyone, or kept evil in his heart. Frank Lloyd Wright was a deeply religious man, but not in the usual way. He freely accepted all religions. When he retired at night he would sometimes say this prayer to himself: "If I die as I sleep tonight—may God keep my soul. . . ."

He wrote steadily and lectured to the faculty and student body every Sunday morning. He gave generously of his time to vast numbers of people, regardless of whether they were rich or poor, had talent or had none, or whether they

Mr. and Mrs. Wright, Easter, 1959

View of Taliesin East—Spring Green, Wisconsin

Allen Davison

were curiosity seekers or genuine admirers. He pored for numberless hours over his drawings and those of the student-apprentices.

As he had created with Mrs. Wright his beloved school, the Taliesin Fellowship—unique in the world today—so now, according to his wish, his wife continues with the momentum that only inspired leadership can bring. His ideas of the principles of organic architecture are being carried on by a highly trained group of architects who have had long experience under Mr. Wright's direction. The group, known as the Taliesin Associated Architects affiliated with the Frank Lloyd Wright Foundation, is headed by William Wesley Peters, many years an associate of the master.

At Taliesin West, building materials are provided and student-apprentices are encouraged to build on their own tent sites in the desert. In Wisconsin, they design and submit for approval their room interiors. Each student may participate in the different aspects of Fellowship life and work. There is the Taliesin choir, chamber ensemble, dance; there are crafts, weaving, ceramics, mosaics, and woodwork. Everyone also shares in the maintenance of Taliesin, of the grounds, the vegetable and flower gardens. A plan for the rotation of work allows each Fellow to partake of all activities.

Alfred Eisenstaedt. Copyright 1956 Time Inc.

Hands of Frank Lloyd Wright at work

*   *   *

Frank Lloyd Wright had an unfailing, intuitive sense of nature, whether in the realm of art, or of philosophy, or of religion. For to him there was no division. He himself was a being whose body and spirit were so closely fused, so interwoven, that there was no barrier between them. He is one of the rare men in the history of the world whose creative genius increased with age. Always far beyond his time, his creative force had reached a zenith in the year of his death, 1959, and he was entering a new universe in architectural imagination. He was never concerned with death, only with life.

Lorraine Lloyd Wright

IN THE NATURE OF MATERIALS

In the East and West, at first, the artificial cave took crude form by use of stone— only in China were they framed of timber and so Chinese origins are lost. The caves were frequently mounds of earth itself. Later, as in Sumeria and Persia, the earth was used more imaginatively by aid of fire—the kiln. Gradually from this early building practice, architecture grew in majesty to the great temple-styles: Sumerian, Assyrian, Egyptian, Chinese, Persian, Minoan, Greek, Philistine, Etruscan, Incan, Mayan and Toltec.

This adventurous life has left on record amazing evidence of man and his gods. Great architectures were thus in time born out of crude cave-buildings to keep man's spirit proud; satisfy his sense of himself. Architecture was then, as it is now, the chief instrument and proof of man's civilizations.

So the architecture of early civilization was raised: either trabeated in form and slab-roofed in stone; or it was pillared, gabled and roofed in wood; as were early Chinese and primitive Etruscan temples. Later, buildings were arched and roofed by that multiple arch we call a dome. Great stone columns—beautiful in themselves—were erected, to be linteled with great stones cut in varied complexes and carved as cornices and pediments while man became more and more style-conscious. Style—then a phase of beauty—soon became a necessity to the civilized human being. With his civilizations came the even greater architectures that we now look back upon and see in ruins. The mind of man has thus gradually evolved a vast and varied dignity of form while developing the abstractions we call civilizations.

Substantial beauty of form came to adorn the earth—form idealized by the creative mind guiding the hand of industrious mankind. Building had become architecture and now proclaimed man's cherished ideals. Now into his view came not only the thorough-built edifice but more and more appeared the edifice evolved with great art—now dedicated not to his gods, but to God. Thus various races of the world have left behind them a vast potential in these ideas of space embodied by form. We see evidence of man's resolution to live, love and worship with truth, fulfillment and distinction. All this is recorded in these ethnic expressions of titanic man's life on earth—recorded by his architecture. From ruins of civilized cities and monuments, great temples and humble dwellings, we learn the character of other civilizations and so learn about our own.

Primitive grass huts of the South Pacific Islands

Indian pueblo

Indian camp on the plains

Within the universe the mind of man has thus made a world, recording that world by his architecture—his ideal of beauty may be studied as he realized himself from century to century.

We have seen earlier in time this world of nature-building that our fellow creatures, of a lower order of being, have built with organic beauty but built circumscribed by hereditary instinct, while man, out of his own mind, by his vision, was left to create a world of his own in order to enter this great realm of spiritual adventure—architecture. Therefore, man's architecture begins where creature-building left off. There, above creature-instinct, where man's gods begin, we find his creative genius dedicated to great building. There he has put on record the greatest proof of his power—his genius. Thus architecture is the great mother-art of creative mankind.

So we find in his architecture the true measure of his indomitable spirit; see his human power strengthened and his life continually refreshed, protected and enhanced by his vast creative vision. This interior constructive power is his own and by this power we may know him best and understand his ideals. We may now share his varied civilizations whatever their origin, and believe man still potent to create greater worlds. By new-found sciences and vast accumulations of wealth he will learn from this study of architecture not to destroy but to fulfill his love of life with gratitude on earth.

Let us look at architecture as we would look from some eminence to a distant sun-lit landscape, seeing architecture as we would the landscape—in perspective as one vast whole. Then let us go nearer to see the various buildings, as we might go to see hills, rock-strata and woods, streams and seas prescient in sunlight or quiescent in shadow that make landscape what it is—the simplest form of architecture.

Man takes a positive hand in creation whenever he puts a building upon earth beneath the sun. While still dwelling in caves, man learned to make utensils of wet clay, he burned them hard for use. Except for this faculty he was no more than another animal. Still clinging to the cliffs, he made whole caves out of wet clay and let the sun bake the cave hard. And so, ages ago, man moved into his first earth-built house.

Walls, at first of earth, stone or wood, were most important, especially where war was in man's mind—the roof

Outside wall plan—Guggenheim Museum, New York City

Section through shell

Plan of ziggurat

Ziggurat at Ur—temple as it was in the days of Nabonidus, last Semite King of Babylon (556–539 B.C.)

was seldom visible. Later the sense of the roof as shelter overcame the sense of walls. Great roofs were seen with walls standing in under them. Man soon came to feel that if he had no roof in this sense, he had no house. If men displeased him he drove them "from beneath his roof." His roof became not only his shelter but his sense of home.

Now, where this primitive sense of structure was going on, the reality of all buildings for human occupation was neither the roof nor the enclosing, supporting walls, but was the living space within. The reality of the building consisted of the interior space which the roof and walls only served to enclose. This reality was not felt by primitive builders. This interior ideal or sense of the building as an organic whole grows, carrying our more genuine culture with it. This ideal is destined to be the center line of man's modern culture.

Paul Popper

The Potala, fortress of the Dalai Lama, rises over the city of Lhasa, Tibet

The ancient builders went to work—lavishly—upon the walls for light and air. Later in the name of art these wall openings were made ornamental. An architect worked his building, something as a sculptor would work a solid mass of clay—striving to mold and enrich the mass. This exterior modeling became the so-called Western Academic Concept of Architecture. This concept was chiefly based upon Greek and then Roman buildings. Meanwhile the Chinese, Japanese, Persians and Moors developed a more plastic sense of building—less a mass of solid matter sculptured from without.

By "more plastic" we mean the building treated as a whole instead of manifestly being joined up of many features and parts. In organic building nothing is complete in itself, but only is complete as the part is merged physically into the larger expression of the whole.

Materials in primitive architecture were most important. Stone, brick and wood spoke truly of stone, brick and wood. Later builders lost sight of nature in this integral

Paul Popper

The dome of the Madrasa Mader-i-Shah, Isfahan, Persia

sense. The old Persian, Dorian, Ionic and Byzantine are all ancient origins of vast importance. All are tributary to our view of architecture as proceeding from one common stock. We may begin with those great architectures in view from about 1000 B.C. to about 1300 A.D. A period of time in which the greatest buildings of the world, traces of which are still visible, arose out of the soul and the soil of what we call civilization: considering civilizations as original cultural impulses.

Mayan and Egyptian architecture have more in common where elemental greatness is concerned than many other cultures. In the Mayan we see a grand simplicity of concept and form probably nearer elemental architecture than anything recorded anywhere else. Next would come early Chinese. In both Mayan and Chinese there was an assertion of form that could only have proceeded from the purest kinship to elemental nature. Egyptian architecture, pyramid and obelisk excepted, has a sensuous

Bruce Pfeiffer

Gothic pinnacles of Mont St. Michel
looking down at surrounding mud flats

Interior showing nave and choir of Mont St. Michel

Bruce Pfeiffer

Mont St. Michel from the causeway—13th century and later

smoothness and comparative elegance inspired by the sensuous human figure. It was a noble kind of stone flesh. The Chinese on the other hand was an ethereal architecture. And yet all seem to acknowledge kinship to each other whether Mayan, Egyptian or Chinese.

The Persian sense of scale was large and lofty and he preserved it by never exaggerating the scale of his exquisite details. Perhaps Persian architecture was origin and end of a quality of the spirit—a feeling for the abstract as form in architecture gradually lost—and never to be surpassed unless the ideal of architecture as organic now reaches logical but passionate expression in the years to come.

We see in looking back upon this vast homogeneous human record that the human race under primitive conditions built most nobly when limitations were greatest and therefore most was required of the imagination.

Plan of Price Tower

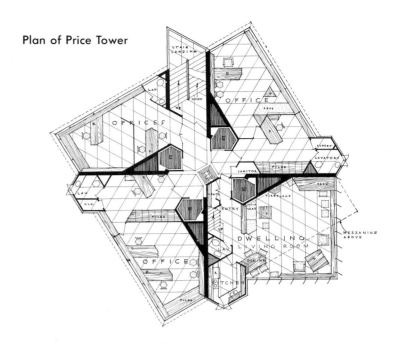

Price Tower—Bartlesville, Oklahoma, 1953

Time Magazine—A. Y. Owen

Section of Price Tower

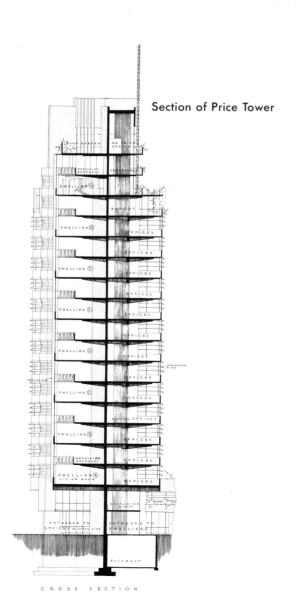

VIEW FROM THE SOUTH

BUILDING FOR THE H.C. PRICE CO.

BARTLESVILLE, OKLAHOMA

FRANK LLOYD WRIGHT ARCHITECT

STONE

Nature continuously shows man the science of a remarkable economy of structure in her mineral constructions that go with the unspoiled character everywhere apparent in nature forms. Her great striated and stratified masses lie noble and quiet or rise with majesty above the desert floor. Great nature-masonry is piled up into ranges of mountains that seem to utter their own form of language.

By nature man desired to build and architecture became, by way of this desire, the greatest proof on earth of man's greatness, his right to be born, to inherit the earth. By innate animal instinct or intuition, he gained ideas of form from those natural forms around him.

Stone is now the oldest of architectural materials on record. From Mayan masonry to Stonehenge, that rude stone architecture of the Druid-bards of whom Taliesin was one, down the ages to the intensely implicated and complicated tracery of the Goths—stone was often allowed to be stone.

Man first used stone as he found it in nature to form primitive shelters. Rock caves in the sides of cliffs were the simplest of all, used just as they were found. Deep canyons could be guarded and gave protection from constantly warring enemy tribes. Rocks and boulders found on the ground were formed into rude huts, but architecture was yet unknown.

At Stonehenge, a circular grouping of rocks created a setting for religious rites. There is a theory that only during the summer solstice could the rising sun be seen through the patterns of stone blazing down on a carefully placed altar. Although there is some doubt as to the authenticity of this theory, the Druids of England still perform a tribal ritual here each June 22. The huge stones of Stonehenge, weighing more than forty tons, were quarried on the Marlborough Downs some twenty-four miles to the north and were eased into place by the brute strength of hundreds of men.

History tells us that religious rituals were in many cultures the all-powerful impetus underlying architecture. The majesty that is architecture arose first to express religion with a sense of style, form, and often exquisite beauty.

Stonehenge—ancient
temple site,
southern England

Mansell Collection

Stone in nature

B. Evans

Stone as a building material, as human hands begin upon it, stonecraft, becomes a shapely block. It is true to square and level so one block may rest securely upon another block and great weight may be carried to greater heights. We refer to such masses as masonry.

Stone may show a natural face in the wall, or a face characteristic of the tool used to shape it. It may be flatly smoothed, then sometimes honed and polished. But walls of stone always take on the character of the surface left by the mason's use of his tools. The character of the wall-surface will also be determined by the kind of stone and the kind of architect. But, most of all, its character will be determined by the nature of the stone itself.

The Byzantine building was more nobly stone than any Gothic architecture—but less spiritually so than the Mayan. St. Sophia is probably the greatest remaining example of the architecture of Byzantium. The Byzantine sense of form seems neither East nor West. It belongs to both: a transition architecture, lost in antiquity.

Ancient Egyptians were the unrivaled master builders of stone temples and tombs. Throughout centuries mankind has stood in awe and wonder at these structures, built of huge stone blocks, or carved out of stone where it stood, as were the funeral temples in the mountainsides. The stepped pyramids of Zoser with the surrounding temples at Saqqara were executed of stone quarried far up the Nile. These buildings are still admired for their dramatic reserve. The

The Pyramids of Khefren at Gizeh— more than 4000 years old and essentially unchanged. Aswan granite blocks in the foreground once sheathed the pyramids

Thrones of Heaven and Earth—Thames and Hudson

Thrones of Heaven and Earth— Thames and Hudson

Saqqara—Pyramid of Zoser by architect Imhotep, Circa 25th century B.C.

Persia—Thames and Hudson

The Royal Tomb of Darius at Nakshi-i-Rustan— cruciform in shape—carved out of the side of mountain near Persepolis, 5th century B.C.

B. Evans

Mosque of Sultan Ahmet, Constantinople

pyramids of Khefren at Gizeh have remained essentially unchanged for more than two thousand years. Time has stripped away almost all the facing of Aswan granite which once sheathed the pyramids and reflected the rays of the Sun God which they symbolized. Egypt's relentless desert, her intricate and highly developed theocracy and her belief in immortality are all evident in her great architecture. The instant that this powerful system and ideal were shattered, art fell into a decline.

At Constantinople, in the sixth century, architecture once again flourished. The fervent inspiration of Christianity, combined with the nearby elements of Persian architecture and engineering, produced St. Sophia. The Emperor Justinian commissioned St. Sophia to be a monument that would surpass all existing temples in size, design, decoration, magnificence and speed of execution. A great central dome, 107 feet in diameter, is surrounded by smaller domes, arches and stained-glass windows. It is supported by pendentives rising from four massive piers with the walls enlivened by veneered marble and gold-backed glass mosaic. The minarets usually associated with the Byzantine Architecture of the East were added much later, following the invasion of the Turks, who converted St. Sophia from a basilica to a mosque. St. Sophia and the Mosque of Sultan Ahmet are two of the most striking existing examples of Byzantine architecture.

Horus, prehistoric Egyptian hawk-headed God of Day

Thames and Hudson
—*Thrones of Heaven and Earth*

66

The stick in architecture undoubtedly came long before stone and stone has suffered through imitation of the stick. Even in the oldest cultures like the Greek and Chinese, great constructions of stone imitate, literally, great wood towerings of poles and posts surmounted by beams richly carved to imitate the carvings of the wooden ones that preceded them and could not endure. The ideas of form associated with ideas of beauty in this use of wood, took the more enduring material stone and foolishly enslaved it to the idea of the ornamented stick.

The Greeks abused stone shamefully. They did not understand its nature except as something to be painted or gilded out of existence. Nor had the Roman architects any feeling about stone; their engineers had—but there were few large stones. The Roman architects cut their prizes into imitations of wood cornices to please the cultured taste of the period and invented the arch to get along with small stones for construction.

Paul Popper

Greek theater—Epidaurus, Greece, 4th century B.C.

R.I.B.A.

Corinthian Column Head— Tholos, Greece, 4th century B.C.

Drama and the mysteries played an important role in the life of the ancient Greeks. Their outdoor amphitheaters show how well the Greeks adapted a simple stone form of rising tiers and half-circle seating around a circular stage to the contours of steeply sloping hills. The Greeks in their temple architecture built structures of stone in the style of earlier wooden buildings. In spite of this imitation of wood, the Parthenon with its Doric columns and the Erechtheion

Maison Carrée—Nîmes, France, 1st century B.C.

Mansell Collection

Paul Popper

Parthenon—5th century B.C.

Roman arena—Arles, France

Bruce Pfeiffer

Paul Popper

Roman arch—Septimus Severus, 3rd century A.D.

Taurgo

Colosseum—Rome, Italy, 1st century A.D.

with its Ionic columns are among the many Greek temples that have influenced building for over two thousand years. But by the time that the Acropolis rose above Athens, the Greeks had lost the great art of architecture. The genius of Greek culture then was best expressed by her poets, dramatists, philosophers, sculptors and pottery makers.

Rome imitated Greece in many ways, but the Romans never possessed that certain refinement of line, balance of proportion and clarity of thought that were emphatically Greek. Yet we must attribute to the Romans the fine engineering development of the arch. Upon such engineering feats Romans continued to veneer the affectations of the Greeks, with columns that support nothing and in friezes and sculpture that all but disguise arches and vaults.

In aqueducts, such as the Pont du Gard, the Roman arch came to its full glory. The lower arches support a roadway across the River Gard even to this day, and the upper arches carried water to cities and towns for many centuries.

The Roman arenas made extensive use of the arch and are on a much grander scale than the earlier Greek theaters. The Colosseum at Rome and the arenas at Arles and Nîmes bear silent witness to the great skill of Roman engineering.

Pont du Garde—Nîmes, France, 1st century B.C.

Giraudon

Stone has every texture, every color and, as in marble, also exquisite line combined with both color and texture. But most building stone is a clear negative substance like some sheet of soft, beautiful paper on which it is appropriate to cut images. By wasting away the surfaces to sink or raise traces of imagination like a kind of human writing, the ideology of the human race may be carried down the ages from primitive to decadent.

Other stone is hard and glittering, difficult to cut. By rubbing away at it with another stone, the surface may be made to yield a brilliant surface finally polished until its inner nature may be seen as though looked into, as in a glass-transparent. Most marble is of this character. The very nature of the material itself becomes its own decoration. To carve or break the stone surface, then, is a pity —if no crime. But man may introduce alternate and contrasting materials which qualify broad masses. These materials, if harmonious with stone qualities, do no violence to stone.

St. Loup d'Hors—
Normandy, France,
11th century A.D.

Bruce Pfeiffer

Bruce Pfeiffer

In 1000 A.D. after six hundred years of cultural decline had brought about the fall of the Roman Empire, a wave of Romanesque building swept across Europe. The architects used the Roman arch and vault and in many cases even stones from Roman ruins. By adapting these forms they were able to carry construction to greater heights and length and created better lighting. Religious ritual was liberated from the dark mystery of the Byzantine basilica.

Reece Winston, Building Centre

All Saints' Church, Anglo-Saxon
Tower—Earls Barton, England,
11th century A.D.

Bruce Pfeiffer

St. Philibert Cathedral, exterior—
Tournus, France, 11th century A.D.

St. Philibert Cathedral, nave

Morienval Parish Church—
France, 11th century A.D.

Bruce Pfeiffer

Morienval, interior

Vaulting was reshaped to bring out a sense of human scale in Romanesque cathedrals, a beauty of proportion. This was primarily a stone architecture, though some examples may be found built of brick or terra cotta. Many unique variations of style were developed by architectural schools native to their regions. Decoration played a minor role in Romanesque architecture, but occasionally sculpture was used beautifully and massive walls were sometimes covered in fresco. From these great works Gothic form evolved.

Bruce Pfeiffer

Abbaye aux Dames—Cannes, France,
11th century A.D.

The Goth perhaps made most of stone. But stone became for the Gothic imagination mere negative material, which they used supremely well in a structural sense. Stonecraft rose highest in the Gothic era.

But the Gothic builders then carved the beautiful stone elaborately and executed carving in the spirit of the construction to an extent never before seen in the world. No arris was left without its molding. It was as though stone blossomed into a thing of the human spirit. As though a wave of creative impulse had seized stone and, mutable as the sea, the noble material had heaved and swelled. It had broken into lines of surge, peaks of foam—images of organic life caught and held in its cosmic urge—a splendid song!

The song of stone? No—because stone was used as a negative material neither limitations respected nor stone nature interpreted. Stone was not outraged but neither was it allowed to sing its own song—to be *itself*.

Bruce Pfeiffer

**Notre Dame,
illuminated at night**

Bruce Pfeiffer

Notre Dame, rooftop Angel Gabriel

The Crusades brought about a valuable contact between the Christian and Moslem worlds. Despite continual battles and suffering, the crusaders returned to France inspired by the new concepts of art and science they had seen in Asia Minor. The craft of stained glass flourished and became a French art that has moved mankind for seven centuries. The ponderous stone

Notre Dame de Paris, view of apse from smaller arm of Seine, showing flying buttresses—Paris, France, 12th century A.D.

Paul Popper

quality of Romanesque architecture was too massive for the delicate translucence of the glassmaker's art, so architects had to face the problem of developing settings of stone in keeping with the beautiful transparent nature of stained-glass windows. Their answer is known to us as Gothic architecture. The refinement of the pointed arch and the ribbed vault made much greater heights possible with thin stone supports. The flying buttress allowed the thrust of the high vaults to be carried by arches to piers far beyond the wall surfaces of the cathedral. The walls therefore became screens of glass, radiant in color, within a slender stone forest.

With ardent devotion and inspired labor, the peoples of cities and hamlets worked together to construct cathedral after cathedral until France became the center of white-stoned glory. Although other European countries took this Gothic style and imitated it, the peak of this architectural form was never so magnificently realized as by the thirteenth-century French builders.

Thames and Hudson—*English Cathedrals,* John R. Freeman, Ltd.

Cathedral, moat of Bishop's Palace
in foreground—Wells, England,
12th century A.D.

Cloth Hall—Ypres, Beligum,
13th–15th centuries A.D.

Wells Cathedral, nave—
added in 14th century A.D.

Thames and Hudson—*English Cathedrals,*
John R. Freeman, Ltd.

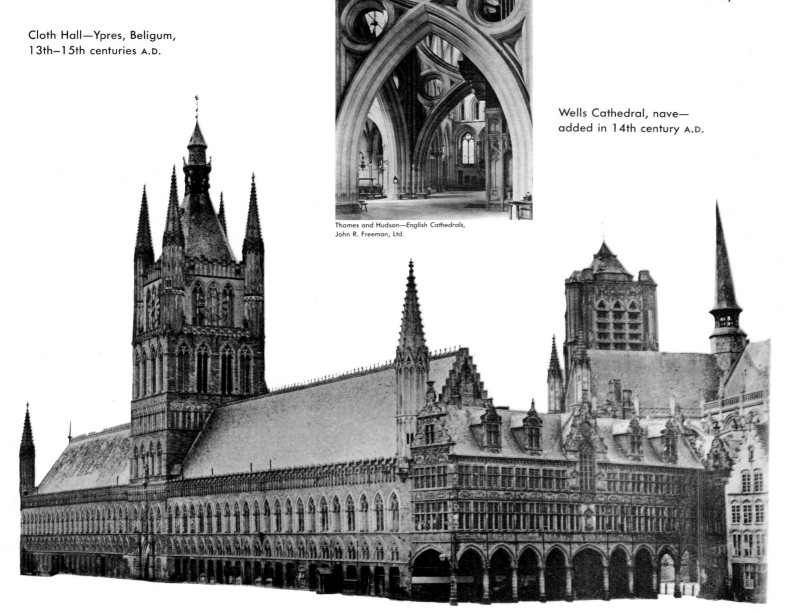

Bildarchive—Foto Marburg

But stone is a solid material, heavy and durable—most grateful for, and so most effective in, masses. A "massive material," so the nobler the masses—the better.

The Mayan used stone most sympathetically with its simple nature and the character of their own environment. Mayan decoration was mostly *stone-built*. And when the Mayan carved it the effect resembled the naturally enriched stone surfaces that are often seen in landscape.

The Mayan lived amidst rugged rock formations contending with a vast jungle-like growth in which the serpent was a formidable figure. The Mayan grew largely by war. He was a great ritualist and a god maker by force. Grasp the simple force of the level grandeur of the primal Mayan sense of form and the Mayan enrichment of it— then relate that to the extended plateaus his terraces made to the mighty scale of his horizontal stone constructions. You will have in these trabeations the sense of the might in stone. Even Mayan decoration was stone-built.

The Inca, Aztec, Toltec and Maya were the great stone builders of ancient Central and South America. At Machu-Picchu, located in what is now Peru, ruined stone structures of a vast scale are found. The Incas carried white granite stones up impossibly steep slopes of the high

Andes and meticulously set the well-shaped stones on terraces, without mortar, to form a fortress, dwellings and connecting stairways.

The Mayans combined a knowledge of architecture, engineering and sculpture in their temples, palaces and pyramids. Their religious building occurred in an epoch when priests ruled with barbaric cruelty. The impact and might of relentless gods are evident in their severe temples where human scale is all but obliterated. Mayan knowledge of astronomy was remarkable. They had an amazingly accurate calendar. They lived and worshiped in close communion with the primal forces of the universe—the ever-revolving heavens and the effects of these changing cycles upon their lives. At Chichén-Itzá an uncomplicated sense of form and simple, sparingly used,

Holle and Company

Borobudur, Central Java, 8th century A.D.

House of the Nuns—
Uxmal, Mexico,
11th–12th centuries A.D.

Bruce Pfeiffer

Paul Popper

Ruins of stone walls and terraces
of the Incas—Machu-Picchu, Peru

Bruce Pfeiffer

Sacrificial lion,
Chichén Itzá

Bruce Pfeiffer

Chichén Itzá (el castillo)—Yucatán, Mexico, 10th–12th centuries A.D.

ornamental detail reflect an evolutionary development over thousands of years. Uxmal, however, built of soft-yellow and pinkish-gray native limestone, finely finished, shows Architecture beginning to degenerate into façade-styles of ornamentation. Throughout the jungles of Mexico and Guatemala ancient Mayan cities have been excavated and more are being found each year. The ravages of the dense jungle growth and decay have left little standing from which we can derive an idea of what once existed.

Angkor Wat, in the Cambodian jungle, is another example of stone architecture devoted chiefly to sculpture and decoration, but this time with a clear and geometrically precise plan.

Elaborately carved capital of the Khymer Empire—
Angkor Wat, Cambodia, 13th century A.D.

Peter Sullivan

So if the architect now will work with stone using the new power which the machine has given him, he will gain a spiritual integrity to compensate him for the losses of the storyful beauties of the period, since passed, when a building was a block of ornamentally sculptured stone.

As a mass material man can now handle stone better and cheaper than ever before, if he allows it to be itself. With sympathy he may bring out its nature.

Man has done this with his machine when he has sawed the blocks of marble and, opening them into thin slabs, spread them upon walls as facings—revealing and accenting its own pattern and color. He has done this, too, when he takes the strata of the quarry and lays it in like-strata—natural edges out—in his walls. He has done well when he makes mosaic of stones and lays them in simple colored stone patterns, a stone brocade inspired by the patterns of the crystal.

Guerrero

Drafting Room, Taliesin West

In 1911 Frank Lloyd Wright built his home and studio, Taliesin, along the brow of a gentle hill with yellow sand-limestone native to southern Wisconsin. This stone is found in the local quarries in definite stratified layers. The horizontal lines accented by these limestone layers gave Wright inspiration for unusual form in masonry. He designed stone walls, chimneys,

Detail of stonework, Taliesin West

John Amarantides

Szarkowski

Garden and terraces, Taliesin East

Winter scene, Taliesin East

fireplaces, piers and the broad overhanging roof to emphasize the horizontal nature of this stone. Occasional projecting narrow stones create a subtle play of sunlight and shadow on the masonry. Stone walls, steps, terraces and gardens reach in varying layers along the brow of the hill, blending Taliesin structurally and aesthetically into its surroundings.

For Taliesin West, his desert home, architect Wright sought the indigenous stone of Arizona. The great rocks of the mountains were carefully chosen with regard to color, size and texture and placed in concrete to form a mosaic pattern in the sloping wall surfaces, reflecting the rugged geometry of the surrounding Maricopa mesa and mountains.

BRICK

We see Tang glazes and Sung soft-clay figures from Chinese tombs—a few of the noble Tang-glazed horses that show Greek influence—Han pottery—and some of the Racca blue-glazed pots and colored tiles of the Persians. It appears from a glance that the oven is old as civilization itself.

Our interest is not archaeological but architectural. It begins with a lump of peculiarly pliable clay in the hand of man. The remains, as we have treasured them in gallerys and museums and have excavated them from this earth, are fascinating record of man's creative endeavor. A record that tells more of him probably than any other —for in it we find not only pottery and building but painting, sculpture and script.

We have hitherto been speaking of "natural" materials. The natural material here is of earth itself. But to produce this material known as pottery, another element, that of the artificer, has entered with fire.

Bricks being fired in kiln

The cities of Kish, Ur, Nineveh and Nimrud once stood on the plains of ancient Sumeria (where Iraq and Iran are now located). Nothing remains today of this early brick construction except mounded ruins, recently unearthed. These ancient peoples fashioned bricks and tiles from native clay; stone and wood were scarce in this area. The crumbling outlines and scattered

Brickmakers, tomb of Rekhmire—Thebes, 15th century B.C.

Skira—Egyptian Painting

B. Evans

Kish, ancient Sumerian walled city on the banks of the Euphrates River—rebuilt in 3000 B.C.

fragments have helped us to recognize the beauty of brick walls of soft beige and red and the brilliant glazed tiles of desert yellow, deep blue and penetrating aqua.

Sumeria is an area where culture supplanted culture for thirty thousand years. They used brick and tile to build Kish, the first kingdom after the great biblical flood, and much later built the great Ziggurats of Ur. Still later the Assyrians built their great palaces at Nineveh and Nimrud, faced with blocks of glowing alabaster delicately carved with records of their civilization. Farther to the east the Persians later built Persepolis and Susa in an area of abundant stone.

The arch was first used in this land between the Tigris and the Euphrates because wide openings had to be spanned with units no larger than brick. The evolution from the Sumerian architecture of great ramps, terraces and roadways to the more delicately ornamented arched and domed architecture of the Persians has created a lasting wealth of architectural ideas.

Arch of longest span
of non-reinforced brick known today—
121 feet, Ctesiphon Palace, Mesopotamia

Mansell Collection

This product should therefore be nearer man's desire—molded, as it is, by himself. What *he* has sensed of the story of his creation, he has put into it. Man sees as he is —sees nothing he is not himself. He is the imaginative geometrical tracery of the Persian and the Moor and the noblest brick buildings man has ever erected. He is the noble sculpture and pottery of the Han Dynasty in China. His is the story painted on the pots and bowls of Greece no less than upon the flowered plaques of Byzantium, or the utensils of the Indian cliff dweller.

His sense of form he took from those forms already made and existing as his natural environment. In his striving for excellence in quality he was taught what to love by stone, reptile, leaf, mold, flower—the book of "trees"— the mosaics of foliage in the sun.

When man, the potter, was at his best he interpreted what he saw. When he was inferior he imitated it. But always, he was his reflection in his ceramics.

Han pottery horse from the
Frank Lloyd Wright Collection

Persian tiles from the Frank Lloyd Wright Collection

Such rudimentary materials as brick, drain and roof tiles are examples of the ancient art of ceramics. After them came decorative tiles, vases and jars—other products of the kiln—to adorn the architecture of recorded history. In Asia and the surrounding countries the ceramic craft rose to great glory. Indeed, China created beautiful vases, urns and sculpture, perfectly glazed and proportioned, for thousands of years. They have rarely been surpassed. An abundance of all types of clay helped China to gain an early lead in the technical and artistic quality of their ceramic work despite the fact that they do not seem to have used the potter's wheel as early as the peoples of Asia Minor.

The heights to which Greek culture rose can be measured in a love of creativity expressed through exquisitely designed utilitarian objects. Legends, histories and social customs are recorded in the delicately lined paintings which enrich the surface of her pottery. Greek ceramics reached great heights in the sixth century

Greek vase

B.C., and from that time through the fifth century B.C. this work can be divided into two main styles: the first consisted of black figures and designs painted on a red background, highlighted with touches of white; the second of red figured designs on a black background. Both basic types of vases rank as paintings, rather than pottery, because of the exceptional beauty of their conception.

The kiln produced elaborately patterned glazed tiles for the Persians and other peoples of Asia Minor which transformed the walls and domes of their buildings into glistening abstract gardens of entwined flower and leaf forms.

What has man to show for brick?—the brick buildings of Asia Minor. We see in the domed buildings of Persia, where the Byzantine arch was still at work, the work of an enlightened people—probably pinnacle to the civilizations that proceeded to the valley of the Euphrates and the Tigris. Persian architecture lifted its arches and domes to full height—when great medieval western architecture was beginning to point its arches in stone.

The Persian loved masonry and by the most knowing use of clay and the kiln on record, he achieved enormous building scale by the way of bricks and mortar. He worked out his roof by way of the kiln as a great masonry shell, encrusted with extraordinary tile mosaics. He made his brick domes strong by placing their haunches well down into massive brick walls. His masonry dome was erected as an organic part of the whole structure. By lifting the sky-arch high, with gently swelling sides, he humanized it completely.

Julian Huxley

11th-century brick arches, Masjid-i-Jami—Isfahan, Persia

Taurgo

Detail of brick vaulting
at Masjid-i-Jami

Mosque Masjid-i-Jami built mainly
of burnt brick—started in 1072 A.D.

The Moslem architecture of the Middle East combines tiled domes, rich with abstract decoration and slender minarets to form structures of delicate and even poetic beauty. Added to them is a combination of pools, fountains and courtyards forming the complete mosque. The domes and minarets are brilliantly patterned with flower and leaf forms which unite nature and building into a scene of exquisite grandeur.

The Mosque Masjid-i-Jami was built in Isfahan, Persia, between the ninth and twelfth centuries. Her two domes are of brown brick and were executed with a noble sense of space and proportion. Subterranean arcades under this

Paul Popper

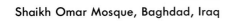

Paul Popper

Shaikh Omar Mosque, Baghdad, Iraq

Golden domes of Khazimein—Moslem shrine near Baghdad, Iraq

mosque have pointed arches of an early Gothic nature but here brick, rather than stone, has been used in a dramatically simple form. The pointed arch was first used in the Middle East and examples date back to the eighth century.

The most striking building in the Baghdad area is the Golden Mosque of Khazimein. The two main domes, the balconies and the tops of the four large minarets are covered with gold glistening brightly against a blue Persian sky.

The Madrasa Mader-i-Shah was built in the early eighteenth century. It is surprisingly delicate in form with two stories arranged around a polygonal courtyard containing open-fronted alcoves. The subdued color schemes contrast with the brilliance of earlier mosques, such as the great blue Mosque of Isfahan.

Madrasa Mader-i-Shah—early 18th-century religious hostel in Isfahan, Persia

The modern contribution to pottery as a building material is "terra cotta"—burned clay. Modern terra cotta has known but one creative master—Louis H. Sullivan. His was the temperament and imagination that would naturally find in this impressionable material ideal medium for his genius. Sullivan's exuberant, sensuous nature and brilliant imagination took terra cotta and made it live. In it this master created a grammar of ornament all his own, astonishing in range, never lacking virility. The Sullivanian motif was efflorescent, evolute, supported by tracery of geometric motives.

In earthenware building we may have, today, the sum and substance of all that the kiln ever gave to architecture. Modern methods have made the complete terra cotta building as definite a possibility as was the Han vessel itself. But terra cotta cannot live on its own texture and color. Therefore it is still mendicant feeding on crumbs from the table of styles.

Town Hall—Stockholm, Sweden, 1923

Taurgo

Ornamental chimneys on roof of the Tudor section of Hampton Court Palace, 16th century A.D.

Central Press Photographs, Ltd.

Stockholm's Town Hall was built in 1923 of soft-hued red brick and is a breath-takingly beautiful building which combines the traditions of both the East and the West.

The original portion of Hampton Court Palace is an important example of English architecture in the Tudor period. It was planned as a lavish manor house instead of the traditional military castle. Originally built in the sixteenth century for Cardinal Wolsey, he later deeded it to his monarch, King Henry the Eighth. Then in the seventeenth century Christopher Wren designed additional wings for William and Mary and made it England's largest palace of more than a thousand rooms.

The Doges' Palace in Venice was built mostly between 1424 and 1442 of varying shades of pink-gray marble cut in rectangles and set in diamond patterns—a surface treatment in stone, emulating brick. Of the two main facades, one faces the Piazzeta and the other the sea. Two

National Buildings Record

Great West Gatehouse—Hampton Court Palace, England

Doges' Palace—Venice, Italy

The Idea of Louis Sullivan—
John Szarkowski—
University of Minnesota Press

Getty Tomb—architect Louis Sullivan, 1890

horizontal bands of Gothic arches form arcades and covered terraces which support the massive upper story.

At the turn of the nineteenth century American architect Louis Sullivan searched for freedom of expression and turned to products of the kiln, such as terra cotta and brick. The strongly delineated vertical accents of the skyscraper were a part of his contribution to American architecture. At a time when this architecture consisted mainly of sterile copies of European styles, he combined a strong sense of proportion and honest use of materials to create a new American form.

The Idea of Louis Sullivan—
John Szarkowski—
University of Minnesota Press

National Farmer's Bank—Owatonna, Minnesota—architect Louis Sullivan, 1907–8

84

Terra cotta lives chiefly by virtue of the human imagination in ornamentation. Let us say now that true ornament is organic—of the thing, never on it. This plastic material develops into its own ornamentation by will of the master. He in turn develops the material itself into forms characteristic of its nature.

There are ways of making a pottery building of this material, admirable in quality and inexhaustible in range of texture, color and shape. The joints of the material become unit-lines in the pattern of the whole, walls solidified by emphasis of the horizontal joint—or by using the pier and mass natural to brick construction today. Brick warrants a more general use which would inevitably cause it to develop. We have brought brick-making to a pitch of perfection never existing in the world before. Our range in production is inexhaustible in texture, color and shape—the material itself admirable in quality.

Facade of Morris store—San Francisco

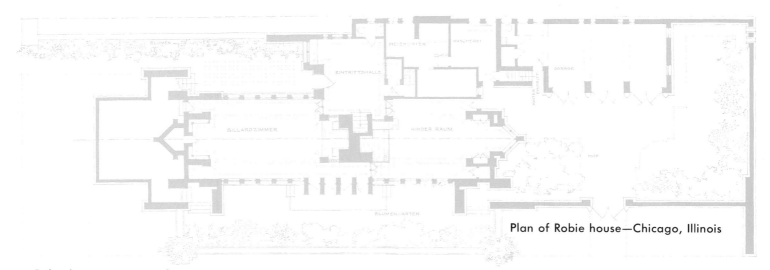

Plan of Robie house—Chicago, Illinois

Robie house—prairie style

Maynard L. Parker

Interior detail Morris store

The sensitive feeling that Frank Lloyd Wright had for the nature of materials is once again exemplified in his use of brick. He attained a beauty of expression with this material, independent of other decorative effect, emphasizing the horizontal line of brick and relating it to the contour of its surroundings. Brick was now no longer a mere utilitarian construction material, but a material of tonal quality with strong plastic characteristics. His use of brick created an architecture that has inspired and given direction to much subsequent twentieth-century building.

The Robie house, built in 1909 in Chicago, Illinois, is an early example of the natural configuration and the simple use of the material—brick—that Wright had in mind. In days when other prominent architects were using elaborate Victorian ornamented decoration, Frank Lloyd Wright designed houses with clean horizontal lines and made the most of the living-working spaces within—a new concept.

A simple brick façade and arched entrance characterize the Morris store in San Francisco —a treatment that is reminiscent of the manner in which primitive craftsmen used brick. Lacking other reinforcing materials, they were forced to create both structure and beauty from this material.

One of the most widely heralded of architect Wright's structures is the Johnson Wax Tower in Racine, Wisconsin. The floors are cantilevered from a central concrete mast and the non-load bearing outside walls are formed of horizontal bands of brick and tubular glass.

Ezra Stoller

Johnson Wax Tower, completed 1950

WOOD

Trees as organic forms of beautiful life have been brother to man on earth down through the ages. The Greeks supposed trees the earliest dwellings of the gods. Zeus spoke his truest oracles through the rustlings of the leaves. And although, in the combined voice of all the poets, the falling leaf has been metaphor of everything that dies, the forest corrects our faith, for we know now that the race of leaves grow off—do not fall off.

The same principle that moves the atoms of the crystal is at work in wood, *organic matter,* more fluid, more plastic than the mineral-crystal of the stone, but—the same. Wood is the flowering of a process proceeding from the same principle as the crystal, though more is left to the individual of any tree species than is given any mineral and even to the mineral species itself. The tree is efflorescent subject of light—imprisoning heat—a growth—extrovert. The tree in this sense is a flower of light.

One hundred and forty inches of rain a year are responsible for the dense stands of towering fir, spruce, cedar, and hemlock growing on the western slopes of Washington State's Olympic peninsula. Here are North America's most luxuriant woodlands. Some of these trees reach a height of more than two hundred feet in wild and primeval forests which have been relatively undisturbed for centuries. Frank Lloyd Wright considered such natural forests as a great heritage and charged future generations with scientifically maintaining and replanting them.

In bogs and mud adjacent to lakes in southern Germany, Switzerland, France, and Italy have been found well-preserved evidences that prehistoric man may have driven piles into the lake bottoms and built settlements of wooden houses on platforms supported by the piles. The opinion that these lake villages existed does not, however, enjoy complete archaeological unanimity.

Prehistoric Swiss lake village

Peter Sullivan

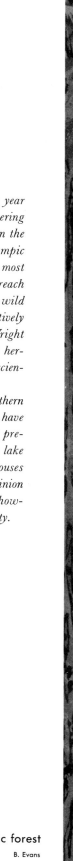

Olympic forest

B. Evans

And yet, of the higher civilizations, the Japanese understood wood best—never outraged it. Japan's primitive religion, Shinto, with its "be clean" ideal, found in wood ideal material and gave it ideal use in that masterpiece of architecture, the Japanese dwelling.

In the Japanese house you may see what a sensitive material *let alone* for its own sake can do for human sensibilities—beauty for the human spirit. The Japanese architect found the forms and treatments of his architecture in tree-nature and heightened the natural beauty of wood by cunning peculiar to himself. The possibilities of wood came out richly as he rubbed into it the natural-oil of his palm, ground out the soft parts of the grain to leave the hard fibre standing—an erosion.

The simple Japanese house with its fences and utensils is the *revelation* of wood. Nowhere else may wood be so profitably studied for its natural possibilities as a major architectural material.

The Hall of Annual Prayers,
Peking, China

Mansell Collection

The pagoda form originated in India, traveled eastward to China and finally to Japan; there it was translated from stone construction into wood. The Pagoda of Yakushiji (680 A.D.) is a structure of three double-roofed stories cantilevered from a central column with enclosing walls to mask the cluttered supporting framework.

The Ise Shrine transcends the influence of China and shows how the architects of Japan developed a style of their own. The columns and

The Hall of Annual Prayers, Peking, China, is one of the best-known Chinese temples. Rich woodwork of red and gold is surrounded by carved white marble terraces and crowned with blue enameled tile roofs.

Himeji castle, near Kobe, Japan

Japan Air Lines

The Shoden, main building of the Ise shrine, Japan, contains the sacred symbols of Shintoism

wall planking are of pale yellow cypress, the roof is thatched. The entire building rises on columns, seven feet above the ground, and is surrounded by white gravel, which offsets its bold unadorned shapes. The shrine has had to be rebuilt every twenty years for the past 1200 because of the deterioration of the wood.

Inherent in Japanese design is the ability to transform structural necessities into sculptural forms of abstract purity and beauty.

The Museum of Modern Art (New York) model Japanese house and garden illustrated characteristics of building uniquely relevant to modern western architecture. These features include post and lintel skeleton frame construction, flexibility of plan, closely related indoor and outdoor areas, and a decorative use of structural elements.

Three-storied pagoda of Yakushiji Temple near Nara, Japan

Garden viewed from the first and second rooms of the Japanese Exhibition house

Post and beam constructions were, by nature, first of wood. The stick is the natural post and the natural beam. Wood is patterned and textured in endless variety by the inherent nature of efflorescence. It achieves color, textures and patterns endless in beauty—perfect in style. Wood is tough and strong, the fibrous natural post and natural beam.

Wood though has weakness. It splits along its fibrous channels with too great ease. The strength of wood lies in a resilient resistance to breaking while bent by loads "across the grain," strength greater or less according to the species.

From the fantastic totem of the Alaskan—erected as a great sculptured pole, seen in its primitive colors from afar, above the snows—to the resilient bow of the American Indian and to the enormous solid polished tree-trunks, upholding the famous great temple-roofs of Japan —wood has been allowed to be wood.

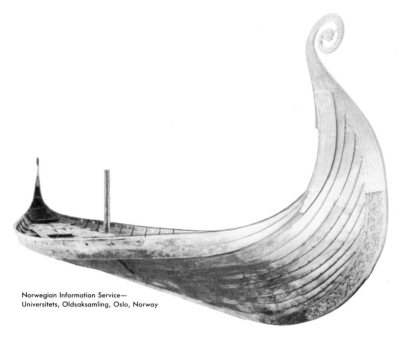

Norwegian Information Service—
Universitets, Oldsaksamling, Oslo, Norway

Reconstructed viking ship—
Oseberg, Norway, 9th century A.D.

Wooden houses—Bergen, Norway

Norwegian Architecture throughout the Ages—Tiegens Fotoatelier

Stave churches of the twelfth and thirteenth centuries were built in the northern forest regions of Norway. They represent a unique architectural development in the use of wood as building material. Examples of these beautiful timbered churches stand to this day in the forest hills and mountain meadows of Norway. Their Viking-like strength makes it difficult to draw the architectural line between the ancient Norse and medieval Christian influence. Their sculptured decoration of carved forest beasts, mythological demons, and winged creatures, much like their French contemporaries—the gargoyles—evince a strong Norse pagan heritage. The Norwegians had a beautiful feeling for related shapes and forms, making it indeed unfortunate that their early wooden structures could not be better preserved. The brave, but perishable, little stave churches of medieval Norway constitute a rare treasure of history.

Norwegian Stave Churches—Normann

Detail of wood carving around the door
of the Urnes Stave Church, Norway

Norwegian Stave Churches—Normann

13th-century Heddal Stave Church—Telemark, Norway

Because of wood we have the carpenter. The carpenter loved wood in feeble ways—but he loved his tools with a greater strength and determination. He loved his tools more. Wood is willing to do what its Creator never intended it to do—another of its lovable qualities. Therefore it is soon prostitute to human ingenuity in the makeshifts of the carpenter. Wood, therefore, has more human outrage done upon it than man has ever done elsewhere, even upon himself.

Orderly piles of freshly cut and dried timber disappear into the mills to be gored, ground, torn and hacked into mill work. They bring a sense of utter weariness in the face of the overwhelming outrage of something precious just because that something is by nature so kind, beneficent and lovely. Machinery has whirled and gouged, ploughed and torn all wood to pieces in the name of art and architecture. The machine that placed this curse upon so friendly a gift is no more than a senseless tool in the hands of man. His ignorance became devastation by way of this tool.

Ceiling of Westminster Hall, London—hammer-beam construction provided for greater spans in medieval times

Half-timber frame construction was used in domestic architecture throughout Europe from the fifth to the nineteenth centuries. Many such cottages, houses, and barns are still found in the towns and villages of Britain. A network of timber posts and diagonals, filled with clay, plaster, or brick, form the walls. They exhibit a simple, human scale; honest use of materials, and harmony with the countryside. The high

Japanese print—sawing wood by hand

Plywood lay-up crew—man at rear feeds short pieces to glue spreader which shoots them into hands of man in center

pitched roofs are covered with thatch or tile. Some window glass was used by the end of the seventh century. Also economy dictated that a two-story design be developed, and by the eleventh century this construction was prevalent.

The twentieth century brought the first use of plywood. Very thin laminations of wood are glued and pressed together under tremendous pressure with each grain laid at right angles to the next. A single very thin sheet of any wood can be applied to create a variety of beautifully grained surfaces. Veneered plywood is used for wall paneling and furniture while the raw product is used for roof and wall sheathing and floor underlayment. Almost every contemporary building, whether commercial or residential, has had plywood used in its construction.

Anne Hathaway's cottage—Warwickshire, England

Street scene—half-timbered cottages, Warwickshire, England

German half-timber house with pegging to secure timbers

What would we have if base appetite becomes enlightened desire and imagination awakes? We may have well-designed timber constructions free of affectation, with satin-boarded wainscots and joints interlocked by beaded insertion, ornamenting the whole. We may have plaster-covered walls banded into significant color-surfaces by plain wood-strips. We may use a plastic system of varying widths of finely marked ribbands to articulate the new plastic effects. We may compound composite slabs of refuse-lumber, glued together under high pressure, faced on both sides with wood veneer.

A most proper use of machined wood are board and batten effects—horizontal, vertical and diagonal—with surfaces rough from the saw to be color-stained or weathered or machined smooth. These define, indicate and relate surfaces. Moreover, such use is true conservation. Wood is used only for its qualities—the tree no longer lost, but preserved in the abstract.

Japanese wood carving from the Frank Lloyd Wright Collection

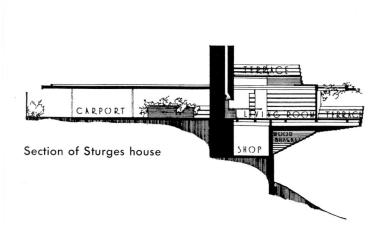

Section of Sturges house

Sturges house, California, 1939

"Abstract Forest"—drafting room at Taliesin East, Wisconsin

Frank Lloyd Wright sought to understand the inner nature or character of wood by employing the material for its own best structural and aesthetic uses. He abolished excessive carving and painting that obliterated the warm hues and interesting grain patterns. His work in wood shows a great respect and love for this rich and varied natural material.

Wright called the hillside drafting room, which he designed in 1933, an "Abstract Forest." It was built by the Taliesin Fellowship. Exposed oaken beams and trusses move in rhythmic patterns with strong wood character and support a series of clerestories from which the north light filters down upon the hardworking apprentices at their drawing boards.

The John Pew and George Sturges houses by the architect demonstrate further his use and handling of wood construction. One is built for a northern climate, the other for the south. In both instances Wright's genius for site consideration places the house in its setting naturally and dramatically by developing the original contour and landscaping of the property. Wherever he employs wood Frank Lloyd Wright combines its aesthetic qualities with its structural capacity, creating a building which embodies the innate beauty and simplicity of the material.

Pew house, Wisconsin, 1940

GLASS

Now let us consider the new resource, glass. This resource is relatively new and a "super-material" in modern life only because it holds such amazing means for awakened sensibilities. It amounts to a new qualification of life in itself. If known in ancient times glass would then and there have completely abolished ancient architecture as we know it. But glass was something the Greeks didn't have; tradition left no orders concerning it. This super-material, glass, is a miracle: light, itself in light, to diffuse or reflect, or refract light itself. Glass surfaces may be modified to hold back or let vision sweep through to any extent.

As glass has become clearer and clearer and cheaper and cheaper from age to age, about all that has been done with it architecturally is to fill with a perfect visibility now the same building openings that opaque, ill-made but beautiful glass screened long ago. Hence the sense of glass as glass has not yet entered into architecture.

The recorded history of glassmaking goes back far into the early dynasties of Egypt and Sumeria. First made into beads for jewelry, glass was later fashioned into vessels and urns. The cultures of Asia Minor led the world in glassmaking artistry up to the time of the first century A.D. *when the Syrian craftsmen migrated to what is now Venice. From the Islamic countries further influences in this finely developed art reached Venice, establishing the city, by the eleventh century, as the center of the industry.*

The constant danger of fire from the workshop furnaces instigated the relocation of all Venetian glass ateliers onto the neighboring island of Murano. During medieval times, rigid laws kept the Murano craftsmen from leaving their island and teaching their well-guarded secrets to other cities and nations. But gradually, during the Renaissance, monarchs and patrons offered asylum to various Venetian glassworkers, and soon the craft took root in France, Germany, England, and the North Countries.

Etruscan glass jar

British Museum

B. Evans

Venetian glass furnaces were moved
to the island of Murano in the 13th century
because of the danger of fire

The machine gives prismatic opportunity in glass. The machine process can make any kind of glass: thick, thin, colored, textured to order; and cheap; and the machine in the architect's hand can now set it, protect it and humanize its use completely.

Glass should be used in such a way as to get its translucence and its beauty as a translucent material and at the same time avoid the glare from the sun. Glass is not beautiful in sunlight. Glass is beautiful only in the shade, in the shadow. It is beautiful there like water. Therefore the glazed openings of the walls, now inevitable in order to realize the sense of interior space in relation to the outdoors, are shaded by wide over-hanging roofs. These openings bring the sense of freedom that goes with the Declaration of Independence. Lighting may be made part of the building itself. No longer any appliance or even appurtenance is needed.

Pompeian glass

British Museum

Glass Manufacturers' Assn.

Blowing glass

Squires, London

Rolling spun Fiberglas

Early Persian glass vase

British Museum

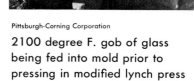

Pittsburgh-Corning Corporation

2100 degree F. gob of glass being fed into mold prior to pressing in modified lynch press

The ancient hand methods of glass molding, blowing, and engraving are still practiced to this day, but advanced chemistry and technology have given these crafts new strength, richer color variation, and new effects. Glass has recently assumed many new uses and purposes through industry and science. The spinning of fibers from molten glass offers thermal-insulation products for building construction.

Design for window in Robie house

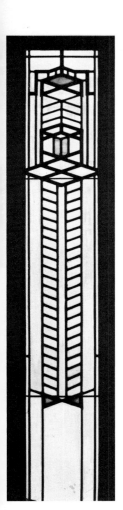

Design for glass window—
Frank Lloyd Wright

The Rogers Lacy Hotel Project,
Dallas, Texas, Frank Lloyd Wright 1946

The Rogers Lacy Hotel, designed by Frank Lloyd Wright in 1946, was to be sheathed in double glass diamond-shaped large panels, the space between to be filled with glass wool for insulation and opaque translucence—an artistic application of a useful but aesthetically mundane product. In the art of glass decoration, in many of his earlier buildings Wright innovated technique and design with his use of glass and metal patterned windows. Geometrically cut pieces of glass, clear, opalescent, or iridescent, were lowered, with metal wires in between them, into an electrolytic bath. Through the process of chemistry these wires built up into supporting rods and securing channels for the glass. These early windows are priceless works of art today.

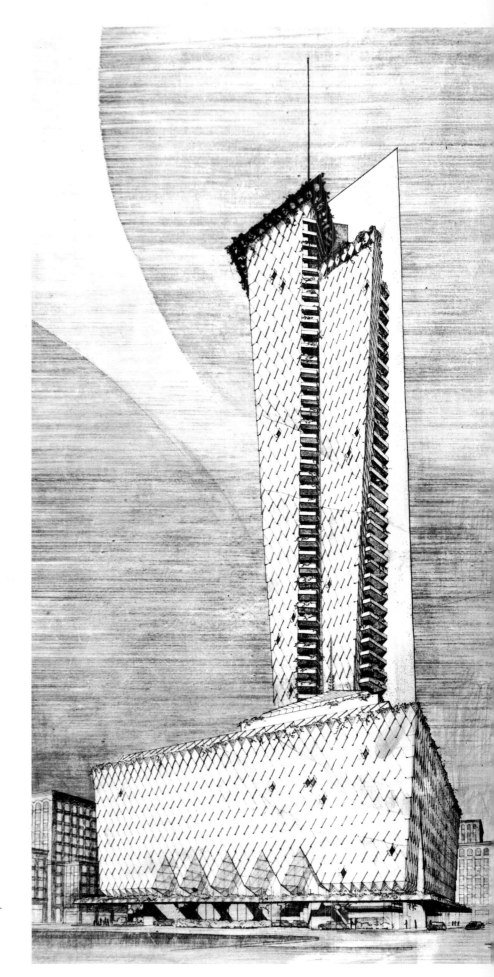

Space, elemental to architecture, has now found architectural expression. Glass encloses the extraordinary spaces which steel, a strand slight and strong as the thread of a spider, is now able to span. By new products of technology and increased inventive ingenuity in applying them to building construction, many superlative new space-forms have already come alive. But, more important, modern building becomes the solid creative art which the poetic principle can release and develop. Imagine a city iridescent by day, luminous by night, imperishable! Buildings, shimmering fabrics, woven of rich glass; glass all clear or part opaque and part clear, patterned in color or stamped to harmonize with the metal tracery that is to hold all together. This metal tracery will be, in itself, a thing of delicate beauty consistent with slender steel construction, expressing the nature of that construction in the mathematics of structure.

North rose window—Chartres Cathedral,
France, 13th century

Giraudon

Bruce Pfeiffer

Interior Chartres Cathedral—view of transcept
from nave showing position of rose windows

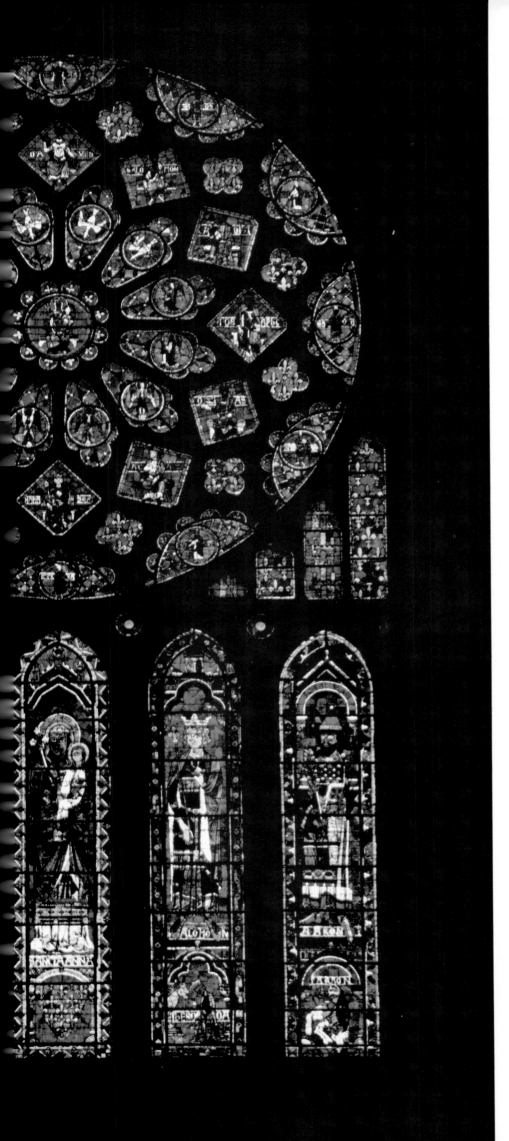

Detail of St. Anna—rose window, Chartres

Giraudon

Notre Dame de Chartres was designed to contain stained glass, to be installed when the cathedral was newly built and conceived as a true two-dimensional decoration. These twelfth- and thirteenth-century glass windows vividly portray the colorful legends, histories, and biblical stories that illustrate the medieval concept of Christianity. A brilliant balance of color within a cathedral of architectural integrity destined Chartres to be the pinnacle of the glassmaker's art.

Many years later the craft yielded to mere factory products, degenerating to the imitation of painted effects in shading and perspective. The clarity of brilliant color gave way to weak tones, combined with a diminishing concern for windows in relation to whole buildings—the art became all but lost.

Chartres, St. Denis, Bourges, and St. Chapelle still are visited by throngs of pilgrims each year who come to view the great surfaces of radiance of these seven-hundred-year-old windows—Gothic architecture's reason for being.

102

Glass and steel together are our modern world, our opportunity—fresh, new. By means of glass open reaches of the ground may enter into the building and the building interior may reach out and associate with these vistas. Ground and building will thus become more and more directly related to each other in openness and intimacy; not only as environment but also as a good pattern for the good life lived within the building.

More important perhaps, it is by way of glass that sunlit space, as a reality, becomes the most useful servant of the human spirit. Free living in air and sunlight aid cleanliness of form and idea; through glass, this is coming in the new architecture. Integral character of extended vistas is gained by marrying buildings to ground levels, or blending them with slopes and gardens; it is in this new sense of earth as a great human good that we will move forward in the creation of our homes and great public buildings.

Interior of transcept—Crystal Palace, built in 1851 and later destroyed by fire

Mansell Collection

Landscape architect Joseph Paxton built the Crystal Palace in London, England, in 1851 using standardized panels of glass and cast iron on a large scale in the fashion of a conservatory. Frank Lloyd Wright, however, realized glass in its architectural sense when he designed the Beth Sholom Synagogue in Elkins Park, Pennsylvania. In this building, glass with its modern companion, plastic, exhibits new possibilities.

The light-letting materials of glass and plastic, made more structural by the use of steel and concrete, have become expressive of the Hebrew faith. In the synagogue the ancient principles of Judaism manifest themselves as never before through the architect's use of twentieth-century materials. By day, the synagogue is a shimmering triangular glory of glass and metal emerging out of strong concrete supporting masses. By night, it reaches into the dark sky as a towering pyramid of light to the world.

Interior view of Beth Sholom Synagogue—Elkins Park, Pennsylvania—showing detail of glass ceiling, completed 1959

Guererro

Architectural rendering of exterior of Beth Sholom Synagogue

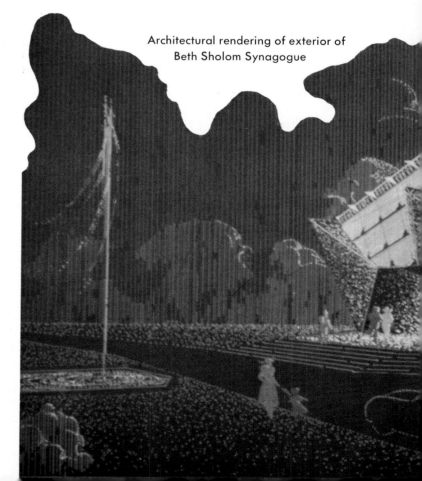

Drawing of the Crystal Palace, London

Mansell Collection

STEEL AND CONCRETE

Steel is epic of this age. It has entered our lives to take upon itself the physical burden of our civilization. This stupendous material—now ductile, tensile, dense to any degree, uniform and calculable to any standard—is a known quantity to be dealt with mathematically; a miracle of strength to be counted upon. Mathematics in the flesh—at work for man!

Steel, a plastic material, thin yet ultimately rigid, rolled hot or cold, drawn into thin strands of enormous strength and length as wire—or rolled in any thickness into sheets like paper, cut by shears into any size. The tensile strength of steel will rebuild the world.

Though steel is cheaper in its strength and adaptability than anything man has ever known before, it has in its nature the need to change its volume with changes of temperature. It also has a fatal weakness—it disintegrates in air and moisture, has an active enemy in electrolysis.

Concrete is formed by mixing crushed stone, gravel, or other suitable aggregate with sand, water, and a cementing material; the entire mass then gradually hardens into a rocklike substance. In ancient times clay and bitumen were used as cementing materials, and the use of burned gypsum and lime dates back to the Egyptians. Concrete and mortar with lime as cement were used

Rapho-Guillumette Pictures— K. W. Gullers

Caracalla—Roman Baths, 3rd century A.D.

Early Bessemer steel plant in operation

B. Evans

Modern blast furnace

Limestone quarry, Tunstead, England

extensively by Roman builders, giving them the ability to create masonry structures of greater length and span, including aqueducts, bridges, and huge public baths. The Baths of Caracalla are an outstanding example of this skill.

The Bessemer process, first announced and described in 1856, gave cheap, usable steel to the architects and engineers of the world. Although now largely replaced by other methods, notably the open-hearth, the Bessemer process was for many years the most important method of producing steel. The process consists of blowing air under pressure through molten pig iron, thus oxidizing some of the iron silicon, manganese, and carbon present to form steel with the great tensile and compressive strength necessary to create the architecture of this age.

Steel may be plated with other metals, protected by coverings or combined with them. In itself it has little beauty, neither grain nor texture of surface. It has no more "quality" in this sense than mud. Steel is a creature wholly dependent upon imaginative influences for a "life" in any aesthetic sense at the hand of a creator.

Yet steel is evident in our life as a thing of beauty, but only where the engineer has allowed his stresses and strains to come and go clean in the members, innocent of any desire on his part to "ornament" them. Steel is most economical in tension—this strand is a marvel. John Roebling ushered in a new era when the Brooklyn Bridge was built.

The principles of construction which find in steel a medium that will support enormous loads with safety, span wide spaces, or support enormous loads to enormous height are, as long as they are kept scientific and clean, the best work we have to show.

New York Historical Society

Lithograph of grand display of fireworks on opening night of the Brooklyn Bridge, 1883

Brooklyn Bridge—perspective made in 1876 from plans of architect John A. Roebling, completed in 1883

Architecture U.S.A.—Peter Juley and Son—Reinhold

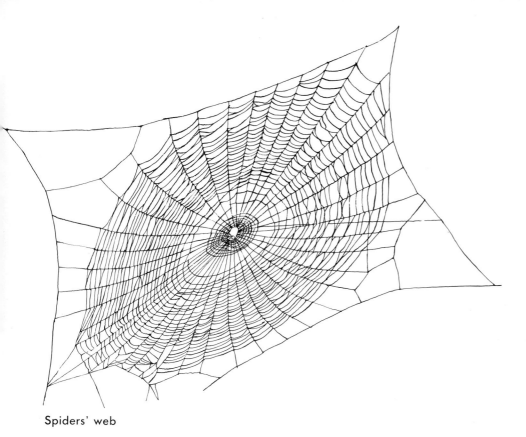

Spiders' web

For many years man has been fascinated by the ability of the spider to spin almost infinitesimal webs which have the capability of spanning relatively tremendous distances. This natural ability of the insect became man's reality in the work of the Roeblings, father and son, who made the suspension bridge an accomplished fact. They developed a device for spinning steel strands on the job into great cables and used these in crossing vast distances with majestic grace. Steel thus was used in tension, consistent with its inherent nature. The Brooklyn Bridge, culminating the lifework of John and Augustus Roebling, was completed in 1883. Though now surpassed in length of span by other bridges it has been in effective use for over seven decades and remains one of the most beautiful bridges of the world.

When the architect has dealt with steel what has he done? The skyscraper and the modern cathedral are lifeless dummies supported from within to appear life-like without. Architects singing their favorite hymns to the medieval antique. Incredible folly! "Tower Buildings," East River Bridges, St. John the Divines, State Capitols; how all of them mock integrity.

Principles of construction now find in steel, the strictly calculable material of miraculous strength, ideal expression as the sinews and bones of structure. The architect has been satisfied to leave the mathematical sinews and bones unbeautiful, although serviceable. It is superstition or plain ignorance to believe these incapable of beauty.

Should not the structural principle be expressed artistically too, with the knowledge of rhythm and synthesis of form of a master musician? Glass is all that is needed after we have honestly insured the life of steel.

Cast-iron bridge at Coalbrookdale, England—100-foot span over the Severn River, 1779

The cast-iron bridge built over the Severn River in England in 1779 by Abraham Darby and John Wilkinson was a very early and rather hesitant use of cast iron on the part of the designers—not yet aware of the material's potential. It is, however, still in use.

Bridge across the Firth of Forth near Edinburgh, Scotland, completed in 1889

The Eiffel Tower, built for the Paris Exposition of 1889, was in its time a truly revolutionary structure exhibiting the tremendous tensile strength of iron and steel necessary to allow structures to rise to almost unlimited heights.

Man's conquest of great spaces was carried further by the great Firth of Forth bridge in Scotland. It was built in 1882–89 by Sir John Fowler and Sir Benjamin Baker and utilized the principle of cantilever trusses with tubular members. This large bridge, with two 1700-foot main spans, was unsurpassed in span length for twenty-eight years. It afforded ample proof of the effectiveness of steel truss construction which was used until the greater economy of the steel cable suspension bridge was demonstrated. The Firth of Forth bridge remains today, in both form and function, a stimulus to the ingenuity and imagination of the engineer-architect.

Detail of Eiffel Tower—Paris, France

General view of Eiffel Tower

Cage of the original elevator—Eiffel Tower

Almost all stone was once a fiery-concrete. The chief difference between stone and concrete lies in the binding medium, which, in the case of stone, is of stone itself, and, in the case of concrete, is cement; but the essential difference between the two is the plasticity of concrete.

Certain truths regarding concrete are clear enough: it is a mass material, impressionable as to surface; it may be continuous or monolithic; it may be chemicalized, colored or waterproofed; or it may be dyed or textured. It is a willing material while fresh, fragile when still young, stubborn when old, lacking always in tensile strength.

We have found how to combine steel as tensile material with concrete as a mass material. Concrete has great strength in compression and combines well with steel, since the co-efficient of expansion of both materials is the same in temperature changes. The bulky material protects the slighter from its enemy, disintegration. A valuable partnership—reinforced concrete.

Space, Time and Architecture—
Harvard University Press—Gidion

Etching (1774) of Eddystone Light, England—slight sea running

John Smeaton, eighteenth-century engineer, triumphed over the sea in his construction of the Eddystone Lighthouse off the south coast of England. Previous lighthouses which had been exposed to the full strength of the stormy sea had been destroyed. Smeaton, locking stones into one another and using a binding material of quick lime, clay, sand, and crushed iron slag, created

a tenacious whole. This was one of the first uses of concrete since Roman times.

Unity Temple, an early interpretation of the monolithic nature of concrete, was built by Frank Lloyd Wright in 1906. In this building, skillfully arranged wall masses with exposed aggregate surfaces enclose the central worship space. The structure is covered by a broad sheltering concrete slab through which light is admitted to the inner area by means of central skylights.

The genius of the Swiss architect-engineer Maillart was applied to the problem of reinforced concrete bridges when he sought to achieve

Unity Temple—Oak Park, Illinois, 1906

Mischol and Schlers

Salinga Bridge—near Schiers, Canton Grisons, Switzerland, completed in 1930: designed by Robert Maillart

Gherardi and Fiorelli

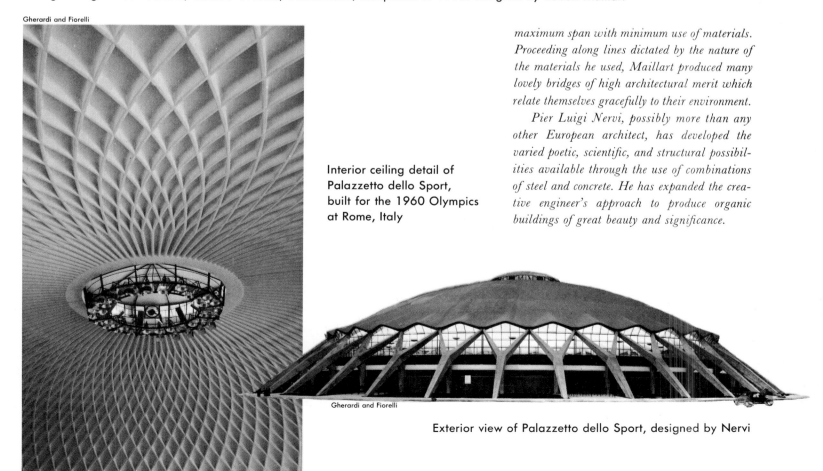

Interior ceiling detail of Palazzetto dello Sport, built for the 1960 Olympics at Rome, Italy

maximum span with minimum use of materials. Proceeding along lines dictated by the nature of the materials he used, Maillart produced many lovely bridges of high architectural merit which relate themselves gracefully to their environment.

Pier Luigi Nervi, possibly more than any other European architect, has developed the varied poetic, scientific, and structural possibilities available through the use of combinations of steel and concrete. He has expanded the creative engineer's approach to produce organic buildings of great beauty and significance.

Gherardi and Fiorelli

Exterior view of Palazzetto dello Sport, designed by Nervi

Millard House—early example of concrete block architecture by Frank Lloyd Wright, 1923

Surely, to the creative mind here is temptation. Temptation to rescue so honest a material from degradation. It is not easy to see in this conglomerate a highly aesthetic property. Cement, the binding medium, is characterless in itself. The essential character of concrete is plasticity.

Unless the flow of the material is considered in the design of the mold and the pattern becomes an intimate feature, casting is usually the end of any plasticity. But a concrete pattern may be designed for casting—featuring this flow of material—that distinguishes concrete from stone.

Easier to comprehend are the new forms brought to hand by reinforced concrete. Waterproof, weatherproof slabs of almost any size may be supported from beneath as a waiter supports his tray on the fingers of his upraised arm, a new freedom. This is the structural principle of the cantilever. A new stability as well as a new economy, due to the use of steel in tension.

Greek Orthodox Church, completed in 1961—Milwaukee, Wisconsin

Offenheimer

Frank Lloyd Wright built a group of homes in California in 1923 which gave artistic and structural significance to the concrete block. Using machine techniques, and with great imagination, he created blocks that could be formed into walls of richly patterned interlocking designs. There are many architects today who continue to use and develop this inexpensive, humble, material.

In 1956 Wright was commissioned to design a church for the Hellenic community of Milwaukee, Wisconsin. Inspired by the Greek Orthodox faith of his wife, Olgivanna, he created a structure of concrete, metal, and glass with gently curved golden surfaces, renewing the spirit of sixth-century Byzantine architecture.

Rendering of Greek Orthodox Church—Frank Lloyd Wright

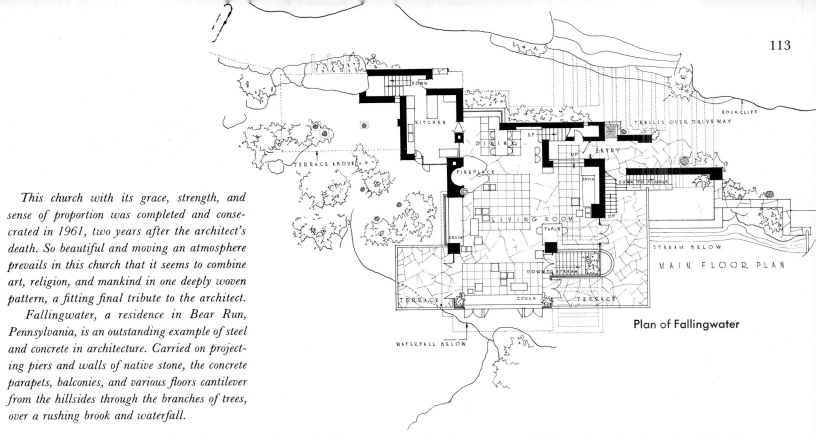

This church with its grace, strength, and sense of proportion was completed and consecrated in 1961, two years after the architect's death. So beautiful and moving an atmosphere prevails in this church that it seems to combine art, religion, and mankind in one deeply woven pattern, a fitting final tribute to the architect.

Fallingwater, a residence in Bear Run, Pennsylvania, is an outstanding example of steel and concrete in architecture. Carried on projecting piers and walls of native stone, the concrete parapets, balconies, and various floors cantilever from the hillsides through the branches of trees, over a rushing brook and waterfall.

Plan of Fallingwater

Rendering of Fallingwater—Bear Run, Pennsylvania, 1939—designed by Frank Lloyd Wright

Detail of Fallingwater

John Amarantides

114

If concrete is to have either form, texture or color, each must be artificially given. Thus it is one of the insensate brute materials used to imitate others. Yet it will hang faithfully as a slab, stand delicately like a Persian faïence screen, lie low and heavy in mass upon the ground or go to work with steel strands for reinforcing.

As a plastic treatment, concrete, en masse, may be printed, as a printer embosses his paper. This would be nearer to its aesthetic nature than any casting. So treated on a large scale, concrete can be beautiful in its own right. There is also the splay or sloping wall, used as a slide from wall into projections or from floors into walls or used with the cantilever slab.

Most usefully then, concrete is a passive or negative material depending for aesthetic life almost wholly upon the impress of human-imagination. This imaginative use of pattern and form is the salvation of concrete in the mechanical processes of this age.

The Fuller Geodesic Dome is a geometrical solution to the problem of spanning large areas with light, inexpensive, mass-produced materials. Based on the octahedron-tetrahedron figure, this type of structure is made of framing materials and can be covered with a skin of paper, plastic, or lightweight metal. It may also be made of folded and externally braced hexagons of steel sheeting. This minimum cost, maximum space, form of construction is still far

Fuller Geodesic Dome as used in the Shaw Botanical Gardens

ahead of many people's ability to accept new ideas and, therefore, is mostly limited to military and industrial use.

Frank Lloyd Wright brought a new sense of horizontal plasticity to architecture with his design for the Guggenheim Museum of Non-Objective Art in New York City. This building of reinforced and sprayed concrete was planned to exclude the crowding and noise of the city. Its interior ascends with flowing continuity some ninety feet upward in an expanding spiral. Each "floor" ceases to exist as a separate level and the entire building, devoted to one purpose as a gallery, becomes one room. But there are variations and subtle harmonies emerging from the spiral theme. The visitor may have an uninterrupted view of the exhibition by taking an elevator to the top level and descending a ramp on which paintings project from the plain walls. This results in an atmosphere of flowing surfaces in which these paintings become part of, rather than apart from, the art of architecture.

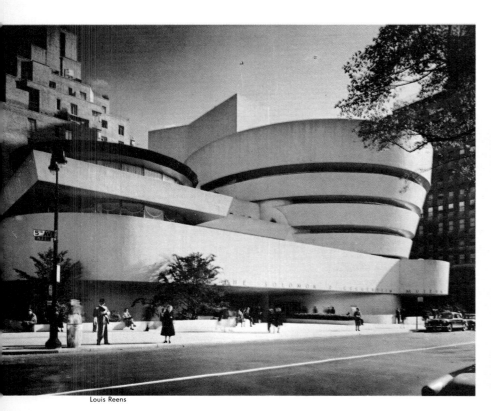

Louis Reens

Exterior view of Guggenheim Museum, Fifth Avenue, New York

Ezra Stoller

Auditorium, Guggenheim Museum

Interior of the rotunda, Guggenheim Museum

THE FUTURE

Modern man has crammed the medieval city of his ancient brother with gadgetry and is now being demoralized by this city not planned for modern uses. The medieval city is still the only city man has; it is his confusion and maybe his defeat—life is overwhelmed.

This ominous trampling of the herd is now a traffic problem in big-city streets; pig-piling of increasing masses of humanity, rolling out to dormitory towns, back and forth—crowds packed into cubicles to work or be entertained in crowds. We hear vain boasts of science as well as government, remorselessly promoting "the crowd"; always more, never less congestion. Meanwhile we boast of the highest standard of living in the world. Society finds itself helplessly committed to these excesses and pressures. Ugliness is inevitable to this inorganic waste motion of precious life.

Congestion, foul air, and outmoded transportation facilities beset the city dweller of the nineteenth and twentieth centuries. Skyscraper cities, created because of and around greatly enlarged centers of learning, commerce, and industry, cramp hordes of people behind airless walls and towers—obliterating all sense of human proportion.

A desperate search for space has caused these metropolitan areas to devour the surrounding countryside, spreading a malignant growth of speculative housing developments, highway billboards, and ugly shopping centers, with an utter disregard for the chastity of the earth or the sensitivity of people, the rape of the populace.

Sunlight, air, and space have been denied nearly all those living in the city, and in many suburban developments there is an appalling sameness and standardization with relentless repetition of stereotyped builders' blueprints. Individuality lost; regimentation moved in.

No social crime has been so grossly and widely perpetrated as the nineteenth-century factory town with home and village crushed into the filth of industrial fumes and poisonous gases. Human beings in these towns live in squalid surroundings with little hope of something better.

Manhattan

B. Evans

A civic conscience is necessary to protect civilian freedom, promising more humanity than was ever promised before. If engineers could have had more sense of organic architecture in their systems and the architects more sense of organic engineering, our modernization of medievality would not be so tragic. Full-scale planning might have saved city life for another half-century. But human crucifixion by verticality on the now static checker-board of the old city is pattern already in agony. The upended street is the invention that made possible this attempt to cage human beings.

Urban-decentralization is now inevitable because of a growing necessity for space; indigestible competition adds to the big-city and despoils the villages. Over-extended verticality is added to the congestion already fashioned on the ground. To offset the senselessness of this inhuman act, the Broadacre City models were prepared, proposing a new space concept in social usage for individual and community building—laid out in accordance with the

Manchester, England, from the entrance to the London and Northwestern Railway, 19th century

Mansell Collection

Frank Lloyd Wright felt that no modern civilization could evolve into a great culture while it condoned the obsolete community. In 1932 he published his book, The Disappearing City, describing the physical and spiritual evils of present-day urban areas and envisioning how democracy should build in its stead. During the next few years he worked on a model-scheme

Mansell Collection

Over London by rail

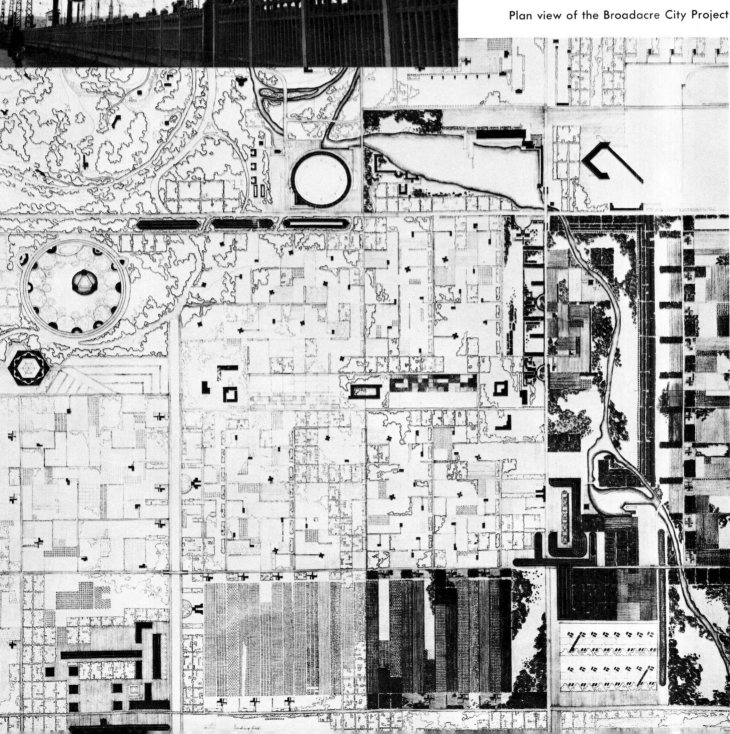

called Broadacre City. He imagined man living on spacious land in the forests, meadows, hills, and prairies but gathering in park-like central areas for work, play, and study. The freedom provided by the automobile would allow him to live in close contact with nature and yet work in a convenient centralized area. Wright planned the skyscrapers necessary for normal commerce but surrounded them with wide green parks and contoured landscapes. He planned schools and shopping areas, civic buildings and motor hotels to be set among gardens and fields, with the entire city taking its character from the landscape and surrounding terrain. He planned for each citizen spacious acreage, in which healthy living and exposure to nature's beauty would encourage a new American culture.

Plan view of the Broadacre City Project

conditions of land tenure already in effect—a new system of subdivision has been proposed. Living will become a quality of man's own spirit.

Thus cheated of general culture, we have little genuine architecture. However, continuing signs of world wide unrest point to a long desired awaking to the needed integrity of an organic architecture.

For the first time in 500 years a sense of architectural form appears as a new spiritual integrity. Heavy walls, senseless overheads and overloads of every sort vanish. Light, thin walls may now rise from cantilever slabs centrally supported on shallow, dry-wall footings. Centralized supports may stand isolated, balancing load against load—seem not as walls, but as integral pattern.

The new sense of interior space as reality may characterize modern building. As interior space to be lived in becomes the reality of building, so shelter thus emphasized be-

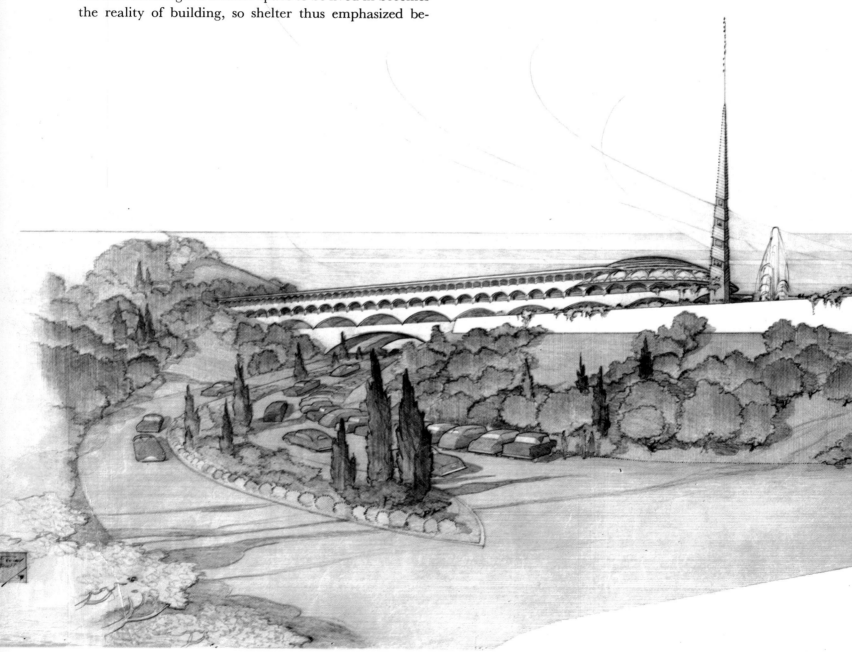

Frank Lloyd Wright again stated his thesis for decentralization in his design for the Marin County Government Center, now under construction to the north of San Francisco, California. Three gentle hills rising out of a pastoral landscape have been treated as an architectural feature, carefully preserving the natural contours of the land. The building was designed to flow between the hills and link them together. Graceful arches and quiet horizontal lines establish a rhythmic motion of sustained continuity—timeless and respectful of human scale. Trees, foliage, gardens, and fountain pools are integral parts of the whole, creating a government office building with a truly inspirational atmosphere in which to work.

The projected V. C. Morris house in 1945 was a tour de force in terms of site and structure. The steep grade of the site gave Frank Lloyd Wright numerous opportunities for the free organization of space and for bold experiments in the use of simple geometric forms: circle, square, and triangle.

V. C. Morris house—San Francisco, California, 1945

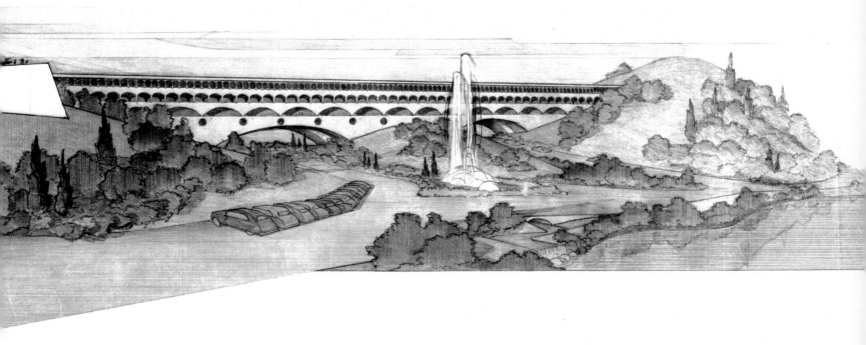

MARIN COUNTY GOVERNMENT CENTE
FRANK LLOYD WRIGHT ARCHITEC

Architect's rendering of the Marin County Government Center—now under construction

comes more significant in character and important as a feature. To qualify this common-sense desire for shelter as the most significant feature in organic architecture, is now of greatly increased importance. Organic architecture sees shelter not only as a quality of space but of spirit and the prime factor in any concept of building man into his environment.

What now is "organic" design? It is design appropriate to modern tools, the machine, and a new sense of human scale. This design is opportune and well within the architect's creative hand if his mind is receptive to these relatively new values. The nature of the machine, used basically in structural design, proves to be a powerful new medium of expression.

Organic characteristics—quiet mass-outlines extended upon the ground levels in becoming human proportions throughout; an appropriate use of materials old and new. Buildings creating a free new phase of horizontality, characterized in early flat-plane prairie dwellings, are

Frank Lloyd Wright created a design for skyscrapers to express both the innate quality of height and the original beauty and simplicity of the vertical line. He proclaimed that a tall building must be tall in feeling and at the same time earth-loving. These structures—the Golden Beacon, the H. C. Price Tower, the Johnson Wax Tower and the Mile High Sky City—were designed as solitary shafts of steel, concrete, metal, and glass to rise in harmony with nature and will point the way in skyscraper construction for generations to come.

Wright's general plan for skyscraper construction was the use of a central reinforced concrete taproot, deeply imbedded in the earth, with cantilevered floors emanating from this central mast. The façade was then finished with copper, brick, or glass panels used decoratively rather than structurally. From Fallingwater (a residence) to the Johnson Wax Tower (a research laboratory) these structures utilize the cantilever and reinforced concrete to create the body of the building with the exterior formed of materials complementing the locale.

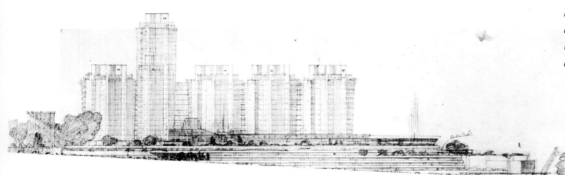

Connecticut Avenue elevation—Crystal Heights Project

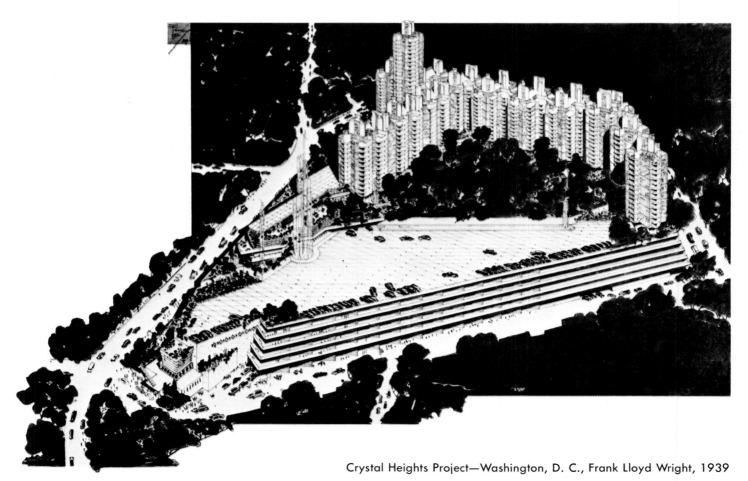

Crystal Heights Project—Washington, D. C., Frank Lloyd Wright, 1939

THE GOLDEN BEACON
CHICAGO · ILLINOIS
FRANK LLOYD WRIGHT, ARCHITECT

also characteristic of the capacity of our new tool, the machine, and of this new sense of human scale.

Organic architecture sees the third dimension never as weight or mere thickness but always as depth—a new structural integrity; outside coming in and the living space within going out. Walls are now apparent more as humanized screens—to define and differentiate, but never to confine or obliterate space.

Organic planning by way of organic architecture is liberation—by decentralization. First principles of organic architecture bring much light upon a new type of agrarian-urban planning. To bring the city and the country back together again in humane proportion requires the vision of the architect in love with architecture.

Completely new character came to architecture by organic interpretation of steel and glass. Steel gave rise to a new property—tenuity. Tenuity is a simple matter of tension—pull. With the tensile strength of steel, this pull

William Wesley Peters, son-in-law of Frank Lloyd Wright and his devoted associate for twenty-seven years, absorbed his principles of organic architecture. He is now chief architect of the Taliesin Associated Architects, a part of the Frank Lloyd Wright Foundation. This group continues the educational and architectural activities started by Frank Lloyd Wright so many years ago.

One of the endeavors of these architects has been to bring from the drawing board a concept known as the Key Project for Ellis Island, which is an imaginative and creative solution to decentralization whereby workers in nearby Manhattan can live in a residential-city. This was one of the last projects conceived by Frank Lloyd Wright prior to his death in 1959. Boats enter a slip in the center of the island from

which passengers disembark and take escalators or elevators to the tall glass apartment towers or onto vast circular terraces. No vehicles are to be allowed on the island with transportation provided in the form of moving sidewalks, escalators, and elevators.

From the great reinforced concrete pylons that

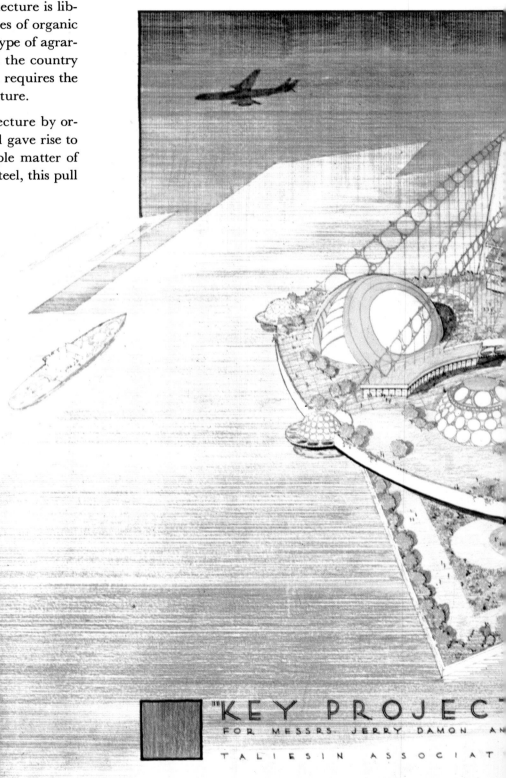

Damon, Doudt Corporation

Rendering of the Key Project for Ellis Island

rise up as the central support of the apartment towers, decorative steel cables hold the large circular terrace with its periphery of domes. In these domes are schools, sports arenas, a medical center, theaters, galleries, a planetarium, and all facets of residential needs and luxuries. Gardens and pools, flowers and fountains adorn the entire project to make the jewel-like city, suspended over and surrounded by water, a beautiful, sunny, and relaxing area in which to live, free from congestion and noise. With its back to the New Jersey coast, the project is oriented to afford a breath-taking view of New York Harbor and the ever-changing sea beyond.

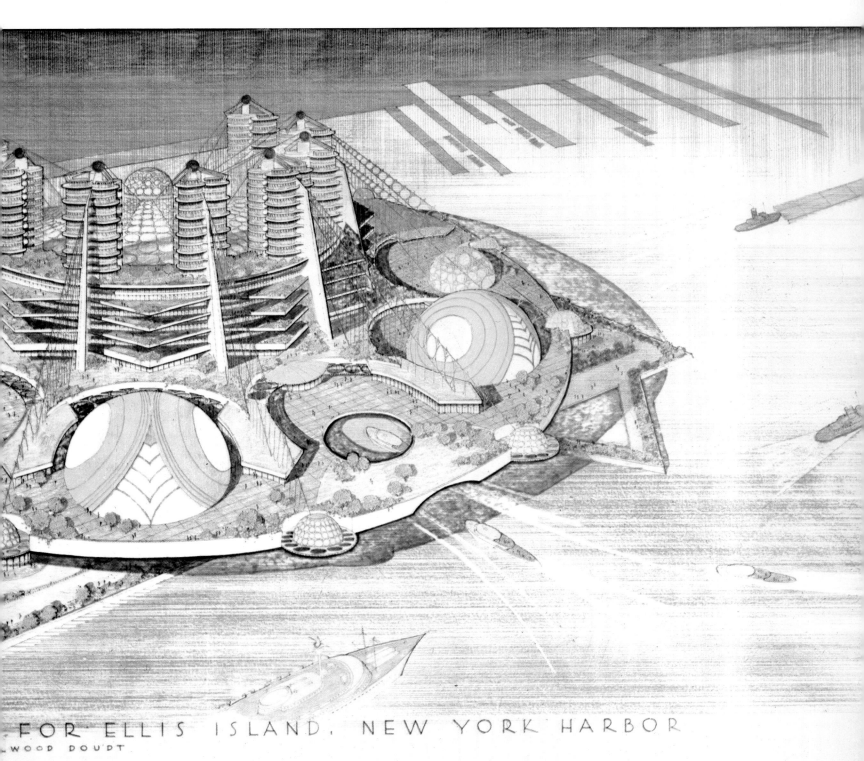

FOR ELLIS ISLAND, NEW YORK HARBOR

.WOOD DOUDT

ARCHITECTS   THE FRANK LLOYD WRIGHT FOUNDATION

permits a free use of the cantilever in building design. This placing of all loads over central supports, thereby balancing extended load against opposite extended load, brought into architecture a new principle in construction—continuity, a new elastic, cohesive stability. This is a new freedom involving far wider spacing of more slender supports. Thus architecture arrived at construction from within rather than from without.

Everywhere the abuses of machine-power, the gigantic property interests, cast ominous shadows upon defenseless human interests. The character of "modern" citizenship is a hangover from the animal—and yet humanity begins where the animal leaves off. Man's essential dignity remains only in his intelligent sense of himself.

Fortunately man is learning to see architecture as a basic element of his civilization, and to understand that his birthright lies in that higher nature to which for the sake of his happiness he aspires.

Significant of the continuing creativity of Frank Lloyd Wright was the increasing number of communities which commissioned him to design their buildings toward the end of his life. So prodigious were his efforts that many of his projects have been built since his death in 1959 and some are just now beginning construction. Pilgrim Congregational Church in Redding, California, was the last church that Wright designed. The main sanctuary for 300 people, the chapel for 100 people, and the administrative wing are all based on the triangular module, symbolic of the Trinity. These three units meet at a broad entrance, above which rises a massive hexagonal tower crowned with the traditional spire of the Congregational faith. Mosaic walls of stone and concrete slant solidly out of the earth, creating a firm foundation for the triangular redwood frames which support the roof. Triangular-shaped windows of colored glass which pierce the roof retain the integrity of the design.

Throughout his life Frank Lloyd Wright aimed at creating beauty within the life of man. His architecture stands as the soaring inspiration for a beautiful and sensitive way of life, while he, himself, stands tall among the greatest.

—THE ARCHITECT—

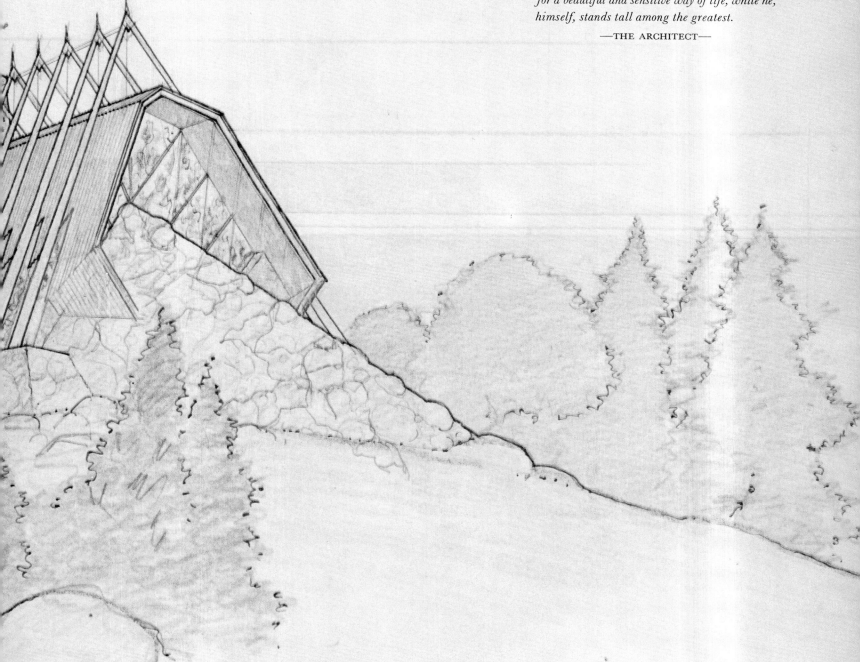

Architect's rendering of Pilgrim Congregational Church project—Redding, California

INDEX

Sunset at Taliesin West

John Amarantides